Life to

'An inspiring and entertaining account of the story behind one of the most exciting charities around for inspiring young people to get out there, grab life and live boldly! I admire them greatly and I know that their work makes a massive difference to the young people involved.'

Bear Grylls – Everest mountaineer, international speaker, bestselling author, Chief Scout and A+ patron

'Built on a vision, and delivered with seemingly boundless enthusiasm, this is the story of a charity that changes lives. Thank goodness for A+! This book brims over with conviction and passion. It's as much an adventure story as a history – and a cracking read too.'

Jeremy Vine – author, journalist and presenter

'Step out of your comfort zone, expect the unexpected and live the adventure of faith . . . A+ is all this and more. Jon's captivating account of the development of their unique adventure youth work is told with a big dose of humility and humour as it takes the reader on their exciting journey, one step, one miracle, one impossibility at a time. Be inspired.'

Jo Gambi – world record-breaking mountaineer and author

'What a great account of God's faithfulness throughout this unfolding story. It began with an unexpected calling and has developed into a first-class youth ministry.

'Christians in Sport had the privilege of working alongside Jon in the very early stages of his work and we were struck even then by his vision, energy and attitude that anything was possible if done for God's glory. His help all those years ago helped pioneer our own Sports Plus camps which have subsequently seen thousands of young people hear the Christian message in the context of their passion for sport. We are hugely grateful.'

Graham Daniels – CEO, Christians in Sport

'*Life to the Max* is the compelling story of the genesis and growth of a history-making ministry to thousands of young people from the UK's inner cities. If you feel called to work with young people, or to make a God-given vision a reality, then this book will inspire and instruct you in equal measure. Learn about the epic adventure of faith undertaken by Jon Cox, his family and his team and be moved to embrace your own faith adventure too.'

Dr Mark Stibbe – author

Life to the Max

John 10:10

Jon Cox

Authentic

20 19 18 17 16 15 14   7 6 5 4 3 2 1

First published in 2014 by Authentic Media Limited
52 Presley Way, Crownhill, Milton Keynes, MK8 0ES.
www.authenticmedia.co.uk

British Library Cataloguing in Publication Data
A catalogue record for this book is available from the British Library
ISBN: 978-1-78078-230-0   978-1-78078-231-7 (e-book)

Cover design by David Smart
Cover, main photo, by Owen Burson: The author at the bottom of
Hell Hole rapid, near Llanstephan, River Wye
Printed and bound by CPI Group (UK) Ltd., Croydon, CR0 4YY

Acknowledgements

Profound thanks to all those friends who have helped, in so many ways, with the writing of this book:

Canon David Winter and Professor John Wyatt, for your initial encouragement.

The very patient 'Script Doctor', for taking my many ramblings and helping to knock them into some sort of order.

The thorough and patient support of so many volunteer proofreaders: Barbara, Margaret, Rachel and the most exacting of them all, my three daughters Anna, Emily and Lucy. Also to Murray for your helpful hints on consistency and accuracy.

Simon and Gail, for their encouragement on the quality and value of our youth work, and for Simon's skill in taking my 'off the wall' design ideas and somehow making them work on screen, and paper.

Huge thanks, too, to the many mentioned in the book, and the many that are not, who have played such a key role in helping us create the vibrant and dynamic team that is Adventure*Plus* today, from such apparently hopeless beginnings. Our trustees in particular have borne the brunt of so many decisions.

Also to Authentic Media for catching the vision for this book and the ongoing adventure youth work behind it; and to Simon for his tireless work on the cover design – as he sought to balance the 'creative ideas' of the author, with the practical requirements and down-to-earth experience of the publishers. Simon you are a genuine 'God-send'. Thank you.

It is evident from the unfolding story that Tessa has been a consistent support and encouragement throughout our shared adventures. Thank you Tessa for your faith, your courage and your love for me and our wonderful family.

The book is primarily a testimony to God's faithfulness from the moment he called us into these crazy adventures.

'To him who is able to do immeasurably more than all we can ask or imagine . . .'

Contents

Foreword

Writing a book, I have found, is quite a project.

Life as part of a team providing adventure youth work for thousands of children and young people every year is busy enough. Family life alone, in a family of six, could easily fill any week of the year. So why decide to add to the mix by getting up in the middle of the night, sitting down at a computer and starting to write a book no one has asked you to write?

This is a question I have asked myself, in earnest, many times over the course of the last two years!

Unfortunately for me, the answer just would not go away and neither therefore would the task.

I was not a particularly spiritually aware teenager, but I did read some biographies of famous missionaries such as Hudson Taylor, Gladys Aylward and Jackie Pullinger.

I was, of course, amazed and hugely encouraged by these heroic accounts of God's faithfulness. Whilst truly inspirational, however, these stories all seemed to take place in a far off land and usually in another century.

The descriptions of places I had never visited made them all the more exciting to read, feeding the imagination and appetite for adventure of a teenage lad; not least because they are true. But I was left with a question: if God has intervened in such amazing and exciting ways in all these exotic places, where is he in my very ordinary world in suburban North London?

We were regular members of our local parish church and I was part of the youth group, but I could not identify anything exciting or particularly challenging from the experience.

So? Why a book?

This story is all about a challenge, to a young man in suburban North London, to encourage people to 'live the adventure of faith'.

It focuses mainly on the early, pioneering, part of the story – what is often described as the 'entrepreneurial' phase. It is a story that cannot be told without describing the many ways in which God has guided and provided, as we have witnessed a truly amazing series of guidance, prompting and clear answers to prayer.

If our work with Adventure*Plus* (A+) can reach a few thousand kids each year, with the encouragement and the challenge to 'grab life and live boldly', to quote our Patron Bear Grylls, then it is my prayer that in sharing some of the adventures God had in store for us, the book will also encourage you the reader.

God does answer prayer in our everyday lives, in areas as ordinary and diverse as North London, the West End and Oxfordshire . . . in other words, wherever we happen to be living!

Perhaps he can only really intervene in clear and amazing ways, however, if, like those inspirational missionaries in another land and another century, we make room for him and start to rely on him, in our busy 90 mph, 21st-century lifestyle.

Jon Cox
Witney, July 2013

For Tessa, such a beautiful and brave co-adventurer.
Thank you for hanging in there when we had no idea
how things would turn out,
for sharing so many crazy times,
and for loving me and our amazing family so much.
You are something else . . . and greatly loved.

Prologue

The unmistakable clunk of a firearm bolt, pulled for action, rudely punctuated the otherwise peaceful African evening.

'*Dageega, anna khawaja! Amshi li musgar . . .*' I shouted.

'Stop, I'm a foreigner! I'm going to the camp . . .'

I stopped dead in my tracks, praying that the next sound I heard would not be the ear-splitting crack of the standard issue Sudanese army rifle pointing at me out of the gloom.

To my relief it was the amazed but aggressive Arabic voice of the soldier behind the gun that spoke into the gathering darkness, questioning what I was doing running through his make-shift army checkpoint at this hour, on the edge of a war zone.

This was a fair question, and one which clearly demanded a satisfactory answer . . . quickly!

Thankfully my first response had bought me enough time to work out a better explanation in the pidgin Arabic I had learned since arriving in Central Sudan the previous year.

I was heading for the refugee camp we'd just set up on the edge of town, and I had decided to take advantage of the cool of the evening to run out there from our compound, rather than taking a truck, but I am getting ahead of myself . . .

* * * *

It was June 1986, and I had been working as a health teacher for a mobile medical unit in Central Sudan for the past eight months. I had left my job as a casualty staff nurse in the A&E Department of the Royal London Hospital, in London's East End, to be trained in community development and health teaching with Emmanuel International, a Canadian Christian relief and development agency near Toronto. After 6 weeks' cross-cultural training and team building, a group of us, including five nurses and a couple of logistics workers, were sent out to join the team in Khartoum.

Our unit was to be based in the town of Damazin, in Blue Nile Province, about a 10-hour drive south of Khartoum.

Anyone who has worked in Africa will understand that our plan to leave for Damazin as soon as possible was frustrated by the lengthy business of obtaining travel permits and supplies.

When we finally had all the necessary permissions and equipment needed for our community development and immunisation programmes, we packed all the gear into, and onto, our two Land Rovers and, leaving just enough room for our unit of three nurses, two local staff and our team leader, Steve, we were off.

The authorities had also arranged for a Community Health Doctor from the UNHCR (United Nations High Commissioner for Refugees) to travel with us to act as a local guide. He travelled in his own Land Cruiser but insisted on stopping at every other village to order *futur*. *Futur* is Sudanese for breakfast, but it was more like a substantial brunch, taken mid-morning and consisting of cooked fish or goat stew eaten by hand with indigenous durra bread and any vegetables or salad in season.

After the third such stop, we'd christened our additional team member 'Dr Futur' but we were starting to get impatient to keep moving.

Dr Futur's impressive appetite was doubtless a great boost for the local economy but it soon began to seriously hamper our progress. Eventually we realised we would need to press on without him if we were to avoid getting benighted in the middle of nowhere. We agreed to separate and that he would catch up with us at our planned overnight destination.

I will never forget that first night in a small Sudanese village. As late afternoon progressed to evening, the shimmering golden orb of the sun descended with surprising speed below the western horizon. Behind us a silver full moon seemed to just appear, suspended in the eastern sky, to cool the balmy evening of my first day in rural Sudan.

Our hosts soon appeared to bring us a delicious supper of hot stew and hard loaves. As evening fell a profound silence replaced the busy banter of everyday life in the village but this did not last long. The growing cacophony of animal sounds, some familiar, many totally new to our western ears, combined to create the backdrop of a typical Sudanese night.

It was the end of a long and eventful day. We were tired and the magical mix of sights, sounds and smells was beginning to take hold of me. I knew I needed to find a place to sleep. But it soon became clear that sleep would have to wait as the grumble of a diesel engine announced the arrival of Dr Futur, who had finally caught up with us.

The glaring beam of his headlights pierced the darkness, as his Land Cruiser burst on the scene, swiftly followed by the inevitable cloud of sand and dust.

A scorpion, a snake and a dog fight

Dr Futur stepped out of his mechanical chariot into our peaceful evening, looking very well fed and pleased with his day's journey. As we sat round a lantern in the thickening darkness beside our *tukul* (grass hut), someone mentioned the danger of scorpions and snakes, reminding us to check our boots in the mornings, and to take care not to wander out in the bush at night with no torch. We had all been drilled in our training about the dangers of the black mamba, which was common in this part of Africa. It was known as the 'two-step mamba' because, once bitten, legend has it that you will be dead within two steps.

Fearless Dr Futur laughed out loud at all the scaremongering and started to regale us with stories of his childhood in rural Ethiopia.

'Scorpions and snakes, szey don't boszer me,' he said. 'I grew up wisz szem!'

We shot knowing glances at each other across the lantern lit circle. 'Yeah. Right,' I could read in the eyes of my Canadian and Swedish Colleagues, 'you grew up with them!'

'Yez,' he continued in a thick, Ethiopian accent that softened every 'th'.

'I remember once lying on my hammock, szinking what is szis wriggling szing under me? Perhaps I should get up and see. But szen I szought, what good would it do? If it is a snake and I get up, it will bite me, but if I lie here a while, it will not be able to open its mousz to bite me and it will not be able to breasz. Szen it will stop wriggling and I can get some sleep . . .'

'So, did it eventually stop wriggling?' we asked. 'And what was it?'

'Oh yes, it soon calmed down, and I got some sleep. When I awoke in sze morning sze whole village was so impressed szat I had managed to catch a black mamba, wiszout breaking its back or damaging sz skin! Scorpions were also very common in our area.'

Tragically we had heard of an aid worker in Northern Sudan who had died after being stung by the venomous black scorpion only the week before. By now Dr Futur had effectively reeled in his audience of wide-eyed *khawajas* and we listened amazed as he related how, if you approach it calmly from behind, you can quite easily pick up a scorpion by the tail, as long as you hold it on either side of the stinger!

Soon the time came for the stories to end and Dr Futur announced that he was going behind the *tukul* for a wash. We all looked at each other wondering if we had just been taken for a ride by this showman and local guide. He came back 10 minutes later, having washed himself down, holding something out for me, as a gift. It was a healthy sized black scorpion! Dead!

'Where did you get that?' I asked, amazed.

'Oh, it crawled over my sandal as I was washing my feet, so I killed it.'

It had been a long and very hot day, but for some reason none of us felt the need to go behind the *tukul* to wash that night! In fact, I was not interested in sleeping anywhere near ground level, so I climbed onto the roof of the Land Rover and spread out my sleeping bag. As I lay on my back, trying unsuccessfully to nestle between the ridges of the Land

Rover roof, I could not believe how many thousands of stars had been lowered towards earth, so close. I had to resist the temptation to reach out, just to see if I really could touch one.

It was stunning . . .

Beautiful . . .

Magical . . .

Until a pack of village dogs burst on the scene just after midnight and my world was filled with the terrifying sounds of the most vicious dog fight imaginable. For about two hours, a pack of perhaps six or eight snarling animals chased each other round and round the Land Rover, barking, snapping, growling and yelping with pain. I'll never know if such violent nocturnal rituals were a regular feature in the village or if it was the prospect of fresh European meat on the menu that was the cause of all the excitement!

One thing was guaranteed. Although I was totally exhausted from more than 10 hours' off-road driving and such a rich mix of new experiences, there was no way I was going to sleep in the middle of that carnivorous mayhem.

The thought of rolling off the Land Rover down into that howling frenzy was the stuff of nightmares; only this one just might come true, if I could not keep awake.

1.

An African Adventure

First impressions exploded across my brain more vividly than any 3D movie, as we drove into the town of Ed Damazin for the first time. As a 22-year-old man who had never lived outside London, I had never seen such sights before: yellow-red earth against clear blue sky, relieved by the dark olive-green of the occasional shade tree; so many of the buildings, either under construction, or falling down – we could not tell which; street traders everywhere selling ground nuts, goat stew, freshly caught Nile perch, tooth brushes made from the splayed ends of sticks; a camel's head suddenly appearing, much larger than life, right up against the windscreen of our Land Rover, languorously chewing; a red and white, illuminated Pepsi vending machine incongruously intruding into this African kaleidoscope to remind me of home.

Our compound was on the edge of town. The large metal double doors, painted pale blue like so many others, were opened as we arrived. The watchman, armed with a big smile and an ageing rifle, let us in.

The house inside the compound was light and airy, with large unglazed windows, a kitchen with electricity and a fridge, and a secure storeroom into which we unloaded two

Land Rovers full of equipment and provisions. This would be an excellent base from which to set up our community development projects, health teaching and immunization programmes in the surrounding area.

Community Development

Damazin was a comparatively new settlement, which had been built, as its name suggests, to support the building of a large dam across the Blue Nile.

From our small compound on the edge of town, we quickly got busy, obtaining the necessary permits to work in the area and introducing ourselves to the chiefs and elders of the local villages where we would be working.

The generosity of the local people was humbling. Whenever we had a meeting with a village chief and his council, they would offer us *futur*, with a spread of chicken, eggs and vegetables we knew they could ill-afford and which, of course, could not be refused. What could we do other than accept gratefully and try to eat sparingly, ensuring there was plenty left for the villagers and especially the children who were always looking on from a safe distance?

We were there to help ensure improved crop yields in the coming years, providing seed and tools and, where necessary, food to tide them over to the harvest. The nurses on the team would also offer health teaching and immunisations for the children. We even helped some villages build latrines to a simple design that kills flies that have crawled on the human waste, before they can fly off and spread germs onto the people's food.

As the work developed it was necessary to head back to Khartoum from time to time to renew permits, meet with our boss at HQ and collect fresh supplies. Sometimes we drove ourselves the 8–10 hours each way, sometimes we'd travel high on the back of the Souk lorries which ply the roads and tracks of sub-Saharan Africa, their British Leyland heritage evident from the Austin, Morris or Wolseley badges prominent above the engine grill.

It was on one such visit back to Khartoum that I found myself in a meeting with a number of the other qualified nurses on the team. Our country director came into the office and asked if anyone could ride a motorcycle. They were looking for someone to run a mobile medical unit riding off-road between villages, providing health teaching and implementing an immunisation programme.

My hand shot up without a moment's hesitation, and I was selected to head up the project. I was introduced to Emmanuel, a trained medical worker and interpreter. Together we were to plan a series of public health classes on issues such as rehydration, water purification and improved healthy diets. We were told to make an inventory of all the kit we thought we would need for the medical unit and to check out the Yamaha XT250 off-road motorcycle that was waiting outside for us.

As soon as we were alone my first words to Emmanuel were, 'Do you know how to ride this thing?'

Emmanuel could not believe his ears. 'What? You said you could ride a motorbike!'

I could not believe how high-pitched his voice could go! 'Well, yeah, I know I did, and I'm sure I can. I just need someone to show me how.'

So began a beautiful friendship and a shared adventure that was to unfold over several months, across hundreds of miles of 'off-road African motocross'.

Unexpected Visitors

As the year progressed, food became even more scarce in the area. A growing aspect of our work included setting up feeding stations for a number of villages struggling to feed their families, whilst also issuing seed and tools to enable the people to prepare for a better crop the following year.

This was about the same time that Bob Geldof was in Ethiopia, hitting the headlines with Live Aid. A very distressing scenario of famine and sickness was also unfolding for the people of Blue Nile Province too, just across the Sudan-Ethiopian border.

All was going well on most fronts in Damazin. We had established good relationships with the local community at most levels from the District Commissioner, the Chief of Police and Medical Director, based in the beautiful nearby rural town of Roseires, to the local people in the main market and our neighbours.

The work was proving to be very successful with local people warming to our team and wanting to learn more about how to prevent infant deaths from dehydration and malnutrition. We had even been asked to research a local region known as the Ingessana Hills to look for one or two more villages for new community development projects. This involved driving a Land Rover through some of the most beautiful hill country, and over some of the worst roads, I had ever seen.

Then one day we received a radio call from our HQ in Khartoum which was to change everything. Hundreds of refugees had been seen crossing the border from Ethiopia into Sudan. No one was quite sure how many people were on the move, but they were heading in our general direction. Our orders were to try to prepare for their arrival.

But how?

We were a small-scale community development outpost, set up with expertise to provide education and immunization. We were definitely not a well-equipped emergency relief centre, with stockpiles of food and medical supplies. Not only were these people exhausted and in poor health, reports said they were thought to be escaping from Ethiopian government prison camps; some were nursing bullet wounds and other injuries and the weakest were already dying by the roadside.

'You are the only agency in the area,' we were told. 'Do what you can and we will do our best to get help to you as soon as possible – give us 3 days!'

Our instructions were clear, but not overly helpful: 'Do something!'

But what were we to do? We were operating in an area that was already struggling to feed its own people. We could not just invent food and supplies to provide for these several hundred people who were reported to be only 2 or 3 days' walk away.

Emergency Relief

I remembered the verse I'd read in my bible reading that morning. It had included some words from the Book of

Isaiah: 'Before they call I will answer. While they are still speaking I will hear.' It occurred to me that all we could really do in this situation was to call the team together to pray. This situation was definitely beyond our control and resources – we needed help.

So I shared the news with the team that we were to expect a major influx of very weak and needy people to our area in the course of the next 2–3 days. We had been assured by Head Office that they would send help as soon as it could be mobilised, in the shape of additional team members, emergency food and first-aid supplies, but in the meantime it was down to us.

As a young team, all in our early-to-mid 20s, this was a huge undertaking and I am sure I was not alone in feeling the weight of responsibility on our shoulders. This was balanced by the privilege and excitement of being right there at the sharp end, with the potential to make a real difference, and the evident need to have to face the situation in faith that God could, and would, provide what was needed – at least until help arrived!

Our prayer was simple: 'Lord, you know the plight of these people better than we can. You know the number of people coming our way and the kind of help they need. Please provide us with whatever is required to care for these hurting people, until further help arrives. Please help us avert yet another major human disaster in this already hungry area of East Africa.'

Time was short and the situation was potentially huge. There was nothing for it but to get on with the urgent business of planning who in the team was going to do what, trying to procure the necessary supplies and building a reception centre for the imminent arrival of our new guests.

Various tasks were divided across the team, which at the time included Steve, our young Canadian team leader, who was also in charge of logistics, four nurses – Mia from Sweden, Bukay from the Philippines, Pat from Canada and me from the UK – and our local team of interpreters.

To add to the intensity of the situation, temperatures in our area at the time made us the hottest place on earth. And this, combined with hot nights, indifferent health and the ever-present risk of insect bites and malaria, seemed to further concentrate the pressure we were all under. It really felt as if someone had turned the heat up on our mission in Damazin!

Although I cannot relate here all the events of the following 3 days, I will never forget how our 'impossible' list of emergency needs was met as our prayers were answered, one by one. To give just one example: there were some warehouses on the edge of town being used to store sacks of durra or sorghum before it was shipped to the more affluent north, where merchants could sell grain at higher prices than they could locally. As food in the area grew scarcer people would start to come to these warehouses to scavenge for any grain that might have been spilled during the last shipment. On a good day, a villager might gather perhaps half a cup of seed.

We were given permission to check these warehouses to see if there was any food left there. We found none but near the back of one of these empty silos we found a stash of military tents, enough to house hundreds of people, maybe even a thousand. No one had even known of their existence but we were allowed to take and use them as shelter from the sun by day and for warmth by night for our travelling guests, who were now only 3 days away. How such a huge collection of tents got there, no one seemed to know. They would have been worth a small fortune if anyone else had found them but to us they were a timely 'God-send'.

We had by now been allocated a flat area of the plain just outside of town to set up the camp. The local police commissioner granted us use of this land and also gave us a sum of money to hire lorries to give the refugees a ride for the last 2 days of their walk – another miracle.

Steve went immediately to the market place to hire several trucks to transport the refugees to the makeshift home we were working to create for them just outside the town.

I will never forget accompanying him with several thick wads of Sudanese pounds, concealed in my faded khaki WWII gas mask bag, to pay the drivers. We drew quite a crowd as Steve, using his impressively practical Sudanese Arabic, bartered noisily with the owners of the souk lorries.

Eventually the various deals were done and Steve left with the lorries, heading south towards the village of Kurmuk, the last reported whereabouts of our Ethiopian visitors. But there were still plenty of gaps in the provision and now that we had sent the lorries we knew that we could expect the first wave to arrive in 2 days maximum.

Call the Fire Brigade

One huge need that still had to be met was that of a water supply, clearly fundamental to the well-being of so many people, in such temperatures; especially if they are already suffering from disease and dehydration. How were we to provide water for several hundred people who were to be based so far from the river? The answer to this conundrum was equally unexpected.

Now that Steve had gone on his mission to assist and retrieve the refugees, it was down to me to coordinate the rest of the preparations back in Damazin. Towards the end of the day, I received a tip-off about a fire engine which had been retired from active duty. It was guarded by a driver who we were told might be persuaded, for a small 'consideration', to take it down to the Nile each day to draw up several hundred gallons of water and bring it to the camp. This, along with a small water butt trailer we managed to obtain, proved to be a workable system over the following weeks, as long as the driver turned up for work, which he did on a reasonably regular basis.

All too soon Steve would return with the first wave of refugees, but we still had no emergency food, cooking pots or bowls, blankets or medical supplies. How could we possibly greet these people, many so weak that their life hung on a thread, without the sustenance they so desperately needed?

The next morning dawned bright as any other, and as we were meeting to check on progress and coordinate the plans for the day, someone came running into the compound with the news that two trucks had arrived in Damazin full of aid supplies, but they were not sure where they could be used and were about to drive on to the next town in search of someone in need of their cargo. We didn't take much persuasion to end our meeting there and then to go and find these guys, who had been sent to the area from another agency, but with no clear instructions. I asked the American drivers what their trucks contained.

'Oh, we got a mix of stuff. Let me see now. We got high-calorie emergency porridge mix for 600 people for 3 days with 2 cooking pots to cook it in and 600 plastic cups to serve it up. Then we got several bales of blankets and enough medical supplies to start a small field hospital . . .'

'I think you have found your destination!' I told the driver.

That afternoon Steve arrived in the first of the trucks, bringing their human cargo. They had clearly endured terrible hardships in their flight from prison camps over the border. Some had been so weakened or wounded that they had died, even after being picked up and given a lift on the trucks.

Communication, Need and Answered Prayer

It was only as we were heading to the police compound where the trucks had been directed that we realised we had one final major problem to address. How were we going to communicate with these desperate people?

Our interpreters spoke English and Arabic, but these people were from completely different ethnic, cultural and national groups. They might speak any one of three Ethiopian languages: Tigrinya, Tigre or Amharic, which none of us understood.

It is well-known in emergency relief situations that if you have a group of desperate, starving people and a stock pile of food, but you do not have the trust of the people – which requires clear communication – there is a high likelihood of the whole situation deteriorating into a riot as everyone tries to get food for themselves and their families. These people were certainly desperate, many of them were armed and they had no reason to trust us. We evidently had plenty of food, but had no way to talk to their leaders to establish a system of fair distribution.

As we drove into the police compound to meet our new charges, we still had no clear solution to this major issue. It was a sobering and humbling moment, when we first saw hundreds of strange and hungry people, squatting and standing in groups in the waning afternoon sun, under Sudanese police guard, waiting for us to take them into our care.

To my UK eye, it was like walking into a TV documentary, but I was no mere observer. There was no channel selector to switch the view. We all knew we had a huge responsibility, and the amazing privilege, of caring for these unknown people. I will never forget the scene. Here were hundreds of individuals, in tribal and family groups, staring back at us, across a hundred metres of African earth, and a vastly different cultural divide.

We got out of our truck and Steve and I were asked to meet the regional Chief of Police in his office before going out to the assembled refugees. He greeted us and we thanked him for providing the money to hire the lorries. He quickly came to the point. He had in the past week arrested four Ethiopian students who had been found wandering in his region as illegal immigrants. As we had so many other Ethiopians to look after, he was sure we would not notice another four mouths to feed. He suggested handing these four guys into our custody, in addition to the large crowd awaiting our attention outside. We said we'd like to meet them before we agreed so he had them brought in.

So we met Kiflom, Kidani, Tadessa and Gabre Selassie for the first time. Each of them was to become a firm friend, and right now they were clearly a 'larger than life' answer to our unspoken prayers: Each of them spoke good English, and all three Ethiopian languages, plus Arabic, and Gabre Selassie was even a trained medical worker!

Through Kiflom and his friends, we were able to organise an orderly and good natured transfer to the site of the refugee camp and set about the urgent task of preparing the first meal. Then the refugee leaders sent the fittest among them to help our team put up tents to provide shelter from the cold before night set in.

God had wonderfully supplied our needs.

If we needed any further evidence, we were to find it in an extraordinary discovery about the number of people we had been sent. Remember the mystery consignment of food and medical supplies for 600 which had appeared on those two trucks?

As we took our register of that first group of refugees, we discovered there were 596 names on that first list, plus Kiflom, Kidani, Tadessa and Gabre Selassie. Food and medical supplies for 600!

It was not until much later, when everyone had been fed and issued with blankets, and our team had eventually returned to our house for some much needed rest, that my mind wandered back to that verse I'd read during my 'quiet time', at the start of this whole incredible episode.

The verse in Isaiah, chapter 65, which I'd then gone on to share with the team could not have been more apposite. Who knows when those tents were placed in that warehouse, or why they had then been forgotten about? Those aid trucks had been sent out from Khartoum days before we had even heard of this Ethiopian Exodus into our area, and yet they had brought exactly what was needed, right to the middle of our town, at exactly the hour of need – almost to the minute . . .

'Before they call I will answer, While they are still speaking I will hear . . .' said the Lord to Isaiah, centuries ago, and through his book to me that morning.

'Mere coincidence,' someone once told me. 'Don't let it build your faith!'

2.

An Unsettling Return

The plane doors closed, shutting out the vibrant heated bustle of midday Khartoum. In an instant the rich mixture of memories and aromas from the best part of a year living in rural Sudan, still so vivid and fresh, were replaced by the sanitized air-conditioned calm of a modern airliner.

As the 737 climbed above the sprawling half built outskirts of Khartoum, the jigsaw of compounds separated by a maze of dirt tracks rekindled a flood of memories – the smiling faces of good friends, the hungry eyes of children, the fiery Sudanese sun setting on the plain behind a 'herd' of Baobabs, in unalloyed contrast to the cool silver moon rising fast on another horizon.

One door closes, we are told, and another opens. As I sat looking out at the dusty, struggling beautiful country I had grown to love, I had a pretty good idea where the next door would lead me, or so I thought. I was bound for Heathrow, then Kings College London, and a BSc course in Environmental Sciences. The plan was to broaden my sphere of knowledge, in preparation for future work in community development abroad.

I had just completed a year working as a nurse and health teacher in Central Sudan. The teaching had often included advice about drinking cleaner water and eating a more varied diet, including seasonal vegetables. The proposed Environmental Science degree would enable me to offer so much more in future. The broader knowledge-base would equip me to give better advice on how to purify stagnant water using locally available materials, and which crops would grow best in the local soil and climate. It all seemed like such a good plan.

As I gazed at the view from my window seat, I allowed my mind to start the process of adjustment, trying to look forward to what lay ahead. I knew I would always be humbled by the courage of many of the people I had been privileged to meet; saddened by the suffering, caused by avoidable inequality in such mortal extremes; thankful for time spent getting to know more about life in such a hard but beautiful land.

Reverse Culture Shock

The initial culture shock of arriving in a strange country, buoyed as it often is by the excitement of the long awaited adventure and the thrill of so many new experiences, is dwarfed for many travellers by the sobering jolt of reverse culture shock when they return home. This is because, although home might be largely the same as it was before, the traveller has changed. Home is now seen through different, more discerning eyes, and in a larger perspective.

'What knows he of England, who only England knows?' asked Rudyard Kipling, from his perspective of a lifetime of travel and living abroad. And so it was for me.

Two scenes are etched in my mind as I experienced the grinding gear change from a simple life in rural East Africa, to all the pressures and benefits of consumerist 20th-century Europe and all it has to offer.

The first occurred in the transfer lounge at Amsterdam's Schipol airport. I had just got out of the plane from Khartoum and was waiting for the final leg of the journey, across the Channel and back to Heathrow. It is hard to describe why the sight of the cheese counter should have made such an impression! It was clean, cool and full of cheese, dozens of varieties of cheese, which is only to be expected. But I had not seen a well-stocked market or shop stall of any kind for nearly a year, since my arrival in Khartoum.

Suddenly I was back in the market in Damazin, Central Sudan, where we had been based. There had been no cheese at all on the stalls, which was fair enough as it was a meat market! But the contrast between that neatly arranged, cold, odourless, well-stocked display, and those warm cuts of meat which I still saw in my mind's eye, laid out on the bare blood-stained wooden tables, dirty, smelly and under a constant frenzy of flies, was stark.

Confused thoughts squirmed beneath the superficial relief of being back in what, for me, was a more familiar approach to civilisation. While at one level it was good to see such a smart, hygienic abundance of good food, albeit in the perfumed setting of a duty-free section of an international airport, my reality was still back with the many friends I had left behind. They did not have access to such a vast array of healthy, wholesome, chilled food.

All kinds of part-formed questions involving injustice, equality, need and greed flitted through my head. Should I be feeling guilty? Was it my fault that I was now standing here in this affluent safe place and my Sudanese friends were not? I could hardly begin to frame the questions, let alone try to find answers.

The second image that hit me occurred a few weeks later – in the run up to Christmas. As I sat having a coffee with my mum in a local Sainsbury's supermarket, a man went past with his shopping trolley overloaded with alcohol. To the western eye he was clearly just stocking up for Christmas, but something in me was shocked at how much money he had spent on alcohol. By now I was getting used to the sight of a family shopping trolley laden with provisions for the week ahead, though even that had been quite an adjustment, but this seemed a more fundamental shift. The trolley was completely swamped with every kind of alcoholic drink I could think of, from 24-packs of beer, to alcopops and vodka, a bottle of gin with small cans of tonic, red wine, white wine and assorted spirits.

I was bewildered by the thought of how much all that must have cost, swiftly followed by the realisation that, from the perspective of a hungry country, it was all totally unnecessary and if appearances were anything to go by, very probably actually damaging to health.

I don't think I've ever been accused of being a prude when it comes to alcohol. I'm not against it in moderation. My issues arose from the juxtaposition between a culture at subsistence level, which I'd grown acclimatised to in sub-Saharan Africa, and the wealth and excess in my native country, which now felt so unlike home and more like a strange land.

There's Got to Be More to Life Than This . . .

I had just over a month to prepare for university life in London and the BSc course at King's College, so life was pretty hectic. It was at this time that I happened to meet a good friend from school. He asked where I had been for the last few years and what I had been up to.

I tried in vain to capture four years' nursing in Whitechapel and work as a staff nurse in a casualty department, followed by that amazing year in Sudan, in one concise reply. When I asked what he'd been up to, he shared that he'd gone into a job straight out of school and had been working there ever since. This may have sounded positive, except that his face assumed a vacant, distant look as he spoke.

He explained that he'd had a weekly paid job and life had quickly settled into a routine. Friday was pay day, so he'd go out on the town with a bunch of mates, often drinking too much and then spending Saturday feeling rough. Saturday evening would be another 'great night out'. Sunday was usually boring or worse, thanks to a banging headache, then it was back to work at 8 o'clock on Monday morning. This routine had been repeated with monotonous regularity week in, week out, for the last five years.

'There's got to be more to life than this, Jon,' he concluded.

His words hit me, hard. Here was a perfectly intelligent guy of a similar age to me, already bored with life. That was wrong!

At his stage in life, he should have been full of excitement about what the day, weeks, months and years ahead had to offer, but at the age of 23 he already felt he was just marking time.

Within a week or two of returning from my own year of real adventure in the beautiful yet harsh reality of Sudan, I found the contrast between his story and my own experience difficult to process. If this was how it was for this friend of mine, the story must be multiplied thousands of times over, for others like him, growing up in everyday suburban UK? It all seemed such a waste and I felt an unmistakeable challenge to respond in some way. But how?

I decided to busy myself preparing to move out of my parents' house, to university accommodation, partly because there was still so much to do, partly to clear my head, but I still could not shake those thoughts out of my mind. Surely life for a young adult in our culture must hold some challenge, some purpose, a reason to get up in the morning? Otherwise – what is the point of it all?

So that evening I found myself praying about it. There were no audible voices or visions of people in high adventure situations, but there was a deep and unmistakeable sense that there was something in this for me to explore. I found myself asking God if this was a prompting from him, or just some crazy notion generated inside the head of a guy disoriented after coming home from such a formative life adventure.

The strong challenge that came to me was to do something that would encourage young people to 'live the adventure of faith'. But what could that mean in practice? It was with a head buzzing with all kinds of conflicting thoughts that I found myself in the bedroom of a standard 'semi' in North London, asking God if there was anything I needed to do with this notion of encouraging people to 'live the adventure of faith'.

Was this an irrational dream taking shape in my own imagination or was this a nudge from on high? And what was I thinking about anyway? What kind of adventure were we talking about here? Would it involve white-water canoe expeditions or knee-crumbling abseils, or what?

An Adventure of a Lifetime Begins

One thing was certain. I had absolutely no experience of anything in the field of adventure activities. In fact the one time I could remember being in a canoe was a complete disaster. I must have been about 12 years old and we had been on a family skiing holiday. Our host, a very experienced Norwegian canoeist, had appeared at breakfast on the Sunday morning and asked if anyone wanted to canoe to church! I volunteered and I managed to tip us both into the swollen waters of an icy river near Lillehammer. And all I had been trying to do was get into the boat!

So I didn't have a great track record with water sports, and I knew I didn't have a very good head for heights either. It was becoming very clear to me, however, that I needed to find a way to calm the whirlwind of thoughts and contradictions swirling around in my head. So as well as trying to pray I decided to get my Bible out to see if there might be some wisdom for me in there. As I took it from the shelf, I opened it somewhere near the middle of the Old Testament, in the book of Judges, chapter 18.

I am ashamed to confess that my initial and hasty reaction was to want to close it again and open up the more familiar territory of the New Testament. I foolishly thought that the

Old Testament would have nothing relevant to contribute, even though it was out of the Book of Isaiah that God had spoken to me so powerfully in Sudan.

I had somewhat absent-mindedly read about half a column, when I came across the following words:

> Enquire of God, please, that we may know whether the journey on which we are setting out will succeed. (Judges 18:5 ESV)

The words seemed to jump up off the page.

I continued with the rest of the passage:

> And the priest said to them, 'Go in peace. The journey on which you go is under the eye of the Lord.' (Judges 18:6 ESV)

The parallel with my situation could not be ignored. They, the people of Israel, were enquiring, like me, whether or not this journey into the unknown was a good idea.

I do not claim to be an authority on prayer but logic told me I couldn't have it both ways. So I couldn't ask God for guidance about an important life issue, and then when I received a disturbingly relevant response, simply pretend it had not just happened.

I had been asking God if I should take a new and unexpected direction, and his answer, through his word, was effectively: 'Go in peace, this journey is under my watchful care.'

As I look back on that brief prayer time, I am amazed how pivotal it was to prove. This was the point at which a brand new life-changing direction began to open before me.

There I was expecting to do a BSc to prepare me for a productive future in International Development when all of a sudden a conversation with an old school friend launches me into a completely different vision for my life – one enabling young people, within the context of adventure activities, to embrace the greatest adventure of all – the adventure of faith.

Good News?

There was good news here, and not such good news. If this was indeed an answer, and not just a coincidence, then it might be very encouraging but it was not much practical use. I was no expert – in fact I was more of a liability in the area of adventure activities. Furthermore, I did not know anyone who was working in this field – in fact I'd never even met anyone who worked in outdoor pursuits or in youth work.

So the good news for me that night was that there was a built-in escape mechanism which ran something like: Okay God, if that word really was from you, then you picked a strange guy to give it to. There must be people here in the UK already involved in this kind of adventure youth work, so I guess there must be something distinctive about what you are wanting me to do. If this really is your voice I am hearing, please provide me with the right contacts to show me where to go or what to do next.'

That seemed a good way to put this whole, slightly freaky, or very exciting, episode 'back in the box'.

'It's over to you, God,' I thought. 'If you want this to go ahead, and it is not just my own crazy notion, then please provide us with the right contacts to show us what you want us to do.'

'There. That solves it, for now. I'll leave the ball in his court.' And with that the light went out and it was time to catch up on some sleep. And that was that, or so I thought.

An Unexpected Meeting

One other ingredient of this strange re-acclimatisation period, back to life in the UK, was that Pat, one of the Canadian nurses from our team in Damazin, was staying for a few days with Tessa, my girlfriend, who had also come out to Sudan for three months to help out in the Khartoum HQ.

Pat had arranged to stop over in London, en route home from Sudan, and two friends of hers, Mike and Chris, were coming over from Alberta to meet her, and take a brief cycling tour on the continent before flying back to Edmonton together.

On the morning Mike and Chris were due to arrive, Pat and Tessa had gone out shopping and I was asked to hold the fort in case the guys showed up. Around 11 o'clock I heard a knock and there at the front door were these two Canadian guys who'd got off their plane a couple of hours earlier and cycled across London from Heathrow.

I invited them in and made them laugh by offering them a 'cuppa'. Apparently all Canadians expect the first words an Englishman to say when you first meet them will be, 'Would you like a cup of tea?' Carefully enunciated in perfect Queen's English. As I was boiling the kettle and making conversation, I casually asked what they each did for work back in Canada.

'I run a Christian outdoor adventure camp near Edmonton,' came Mike's reply.

My jaw nearly hit the floor in amazement. 'That is ridiculous!' I blurted out before I realised how rude that must sound to them.

'Well thanks, why is that so ridiculous?'

We weren't off to the best start. A quick explanation was needed.

I told them about the strange and totally unexpected 'calling' so soon after my return from Sudan, and how only the night before I'd been praying that God would provide contacts to show us how we should build an adventure outreach for young people, even though I had never met anyone involved in that kind of work.

That, I explained, was why I was so amazed that they should walk through the door, all the way from Alberta, Canada, the very next morning.

'Another mere coincidence?' I asked myself, or was it time to start listening?

3.

The University of Life

We got to know Chris and Mike much better over the next fortnight. By the time they had to leave with Pat for Canada, we were all hatching a plan for Tessa and me to visit them at Birch Bay Ranch the following summer. Meanwhile, we felt it was right for me to stay with the plan for my uni course and I was now frenetic with final preparations for my move into student accommodation.

Environmental Sciences was a completely inappropriate course for me to be studying and yet squarely where my sphere of interest lay. It was the perfect next step in helping me become a really useful community development and aid worker in the developing world, so from that point of view it was ideal. On the other hand, A-levels in History, English and Music had done little to prepare me for course units in Physiology, Pharmacology and Statistics. When I saw the title of one of my first year units, Bio-Geo-Chemical Sciences, my heart sank.

My only hope was that my nursing studies might inform the 'Bio' bit, which could in turn help with some understanding of the 'Geo', which might then shed a little light on the 'chemical'.

I well remember the near despair during that first year, sitting somewhere near the back of a lecture hall in Central

London trying to trap a few of the long words I heard from the front onto one of the index cards I carried everywhere with me. Each evening I would sit working through those cards, usually starting at the index of the various basic text books I'd bought, trying to work out what they all meant and how they fitted in to the bigger picture.

I seemed constantly to have no idea what on earth the well-meaning lecturers were talking about. But it was when I realised I could not even understand most of the questions coming from the other students that I began to feel really inadequate.

Although it is quite amusing to look back on this now, the overwhelming sense of helplessness at the time was no doubt made more acute by the sharp contrast between life as a project leader in a very real situation in Central Sudan with life as a student – especially one with very little hope of ever completing the course. On several occasions during that first term, I came very close to leaving and getting back on a plane to Sudan, where I knew I could be useful.

The wise words of a good friend helped me stay on track, when I admitted that I was sorely tempted to run back to more adventurous, yet somehow safer waters. She suggested that 'God usually calls us *into* something – not out of something just because it is a challenging situation.'

Everybody Needs Good Neighbours

It was not all gloom and doom, however. I found myself living in a shared house on Parliament Hill, right on the edge of Hampstead Heath. I don't think I could have asked for a more beautiful backdrop to life in Central London.

One strategy I adopted to help me stay sane in this crazy year was running on the heath and swimming in the open air bathing lakes. Church life was good too, with a growing involvement in the brass section of the orchestra at my church, All Souls Langham Place.

The other occupants of the house were all Aussies and Kiwis, except for two Americans and me the token Brit. The Americans were pretty cool and seemed to be enjoying their stay in Central London. One of them, Todd, a lanky, long haired New Yorker was constantly amazed that our television stations would devote hours to Championship Darts.

I would often hear him in his room late into the night laughing out loud as the commentator shouted, as if he was announcing the opening of a major new attraction: '*One hundred and ay-teeee.*' This was a source of constant entertainment for him and occasionally I'd even go in and watch it with him, or rather watch him watching the darts. I couldn't resist – it was just too entertaining.

I was given a shared room with Stewart, a young Australian chef, cooking to fund his stay in the UK and, like most of the rest of the housemates, disappearing off sometimes for weeks at a time to 'do Europe'. When Stewart was around he and I led a strangely contrasting existence. He would often be up well before me to start his day preparing breakfast in various pubs and hotels across London, and when he came home I would just be settling in for a long evening, studying into the small hours, equipped with index cards and text books, trying to make sense of it all.

This was also probably the most violent year of my life so far. It soon became apparent that every time Australia or New Zealand lost any sports fixture, and I, or anyone else, happened to mention it, there would be consequences. Good natured, but aggressive nonetheless.

Unfortunately in that year the Aussies lost the America's Cup and the Ashes, and the All Blacks also took the odd pasting, but the best result of all was when the Australian Aussie-rules football team took on the Irish Gaelic football team – at Aussie-rules football – and lost! Obviously we couldn't let that one go without comment, and one evening it all erupted and sofas literally flew across the lounge. The ensuing ruck ended with me struggling for breath under the sofa, with a few stocky Wallaby-Wannabes looking down at me, just to press their point.

And so my first year of university life settled into a surreal routine of desperate study just to keep up with nearly every aspect of the course, and a home life that felt like a guest appearance in a well-known Australian soap opera, all thankfully with the backdrop of Hampstead Heath, perfect for stress-busting runs, just up the road to help maintain a level of sanity.

Birch Bay Ranch

As the weeks progressed into months, the prospect of a visit to Birch Bay Ranch the following summer also kept me going through the difficult first year of my degree. Mike offered to sort out a work permit from his end if we could organise visas, and so the prospect of three months in Western Canada, with a beautiful Gibraltarian girlfriend I had hardly seen all year, provided a welcome distraction from the otherwise desperate preparation for end of year exams.

Tessa went out ahead of me as I needed to stay behind to check whether there were any exams I'd need to re-sit. To my amazement I passed all the units and it was with a sense of real excitement that I boarded another plane, this time bound for Minneapolis-St Paul, then on to Edmonton, Alberta, in the borderlands between the Prairies and the foothills of the Canadian Rockies.

I was met at Edmonton Airport by Tessa, with Mike, who'd been with us in the UK a year earlier, and Tim, another of the leaders at Birch Bay Ranch that summer. After a short drive out of Edmonton, we arrived at the outlying town of Sherwood Park, then on into the countryside, and eventually turned off the Highway into Range Road 215. Before I knew it we were driving under the arched entrance of a Wild West Ranch!

As we drove further onto the property we passed a rodeo arena and then down a typical Spaghetti Western small town main street, with all the usual features: the blacksmith's shop, the bank, the general store and the saloon. I soon realised that these were in fact merely facades for the residential cabins for the kids.

This was undoubtedly a place fully focused on having fun, with all the facilities needed for an adventure programme. The property, which was surrounded by a beautiful birch forest, led eventually down to a stunning lake shore, with a beautifully situated camp fire seating area.

There were still a few days before the kids arrived for the first week of summer camp. Everyone was busy with last minute preparations and I received some training for my role as cabin counsellor and leader in charge of the climbing wall! As I had done very little climbing at that time, training included a chance to climb most routes on the outdoor wall, a rapid course in belaying and the system for what to do if a child got stuck half way up, or down, the wall.

I well remember the classic Willans sit harness I was issued. This model, whilst a great improvement on the simple climbing belt it succeeded, is now outdated, which is a good thing as the single strap that stretches from the waist belt at the back, down under the crotch and up to the waist belt at the front, offers absolutely no mercy when you fall! The advent of leg loops and comfort straps has made a big difference to the enjoyment of the sport of climbing, or at least to the art of falling.

The climbing wall, which also had an abseiling face, was just one small part of a very varied programme. We were ideally situated in a clearing in the birch woods, near the end of a high ropes course and anyone walking down to the waterfront to watch the canoeing would also pass the archery range. Then there were the air rifles, arts and crafts, and drama, but the largest activity resource, and definitely a firm favourite with many of the children, were the horses.

In fact, the week at Birch Bay began and ended with a rodeo. Parents would arrive with their children on a Sunday afternoon to watch a display from the stable hands and ranchers and, when they collected their children the following Saturday, they would watch their children take part in various competitions in the rodeo ring, often performing all kinds of gymnastics on horseback.

Camp Fire

As we started to learn the ropes for our roles at BBR, it soon became clear to both Tessa and me that this was a very special place in the lives of hundreds of children every summer. The emphasis seemed to be on giving the kids such a brilliant time that they would want to come back the following summer and return as leaders when they were older.

The campers came from a wide variety of backgrounds. Although BBR was staffed and supported mainly by a large church in central Edmonton, the kids were by no means all from church families, and there was a generous but unadvertised scattering of social care placements.

One of the things that encouraged us was the positive and encouraging atmosphere that seemed to pervade every aspect of the camp, from the mealtimes and activities through to the camp fire and the cabin discussions.

Camp fire was a big highlight. After a full day of activities, and a bustling evening meal in the canteen, we would all troop down to the shores of the lake where a camp fire would be burning before a rough semi-circle of wooden benches. As the sun set over the lake behind, we would all enjoy a mix of some ridiculously funny 'skits', sing what were clearly favourite camp-fire songs and then a speaker would share some thoughts about 'the bigger picture', and life issues relevant to that age group, from a positive Christian perspective.

What most impressed Tessa and me was the fact that camp fire was clearly one of the most popular and eagerly awaited parts of the day, and with good reason. It really was a heap of fun, well run and a fine way to end such a busy and exciting day. The camp fire was followed by hot chocolate and cake back in the canteen, before the children headed back to their bunks, for cabin discussions and bed.

The 'Real World'

There were so many memorable moments at Birch Bay that summer, but I cannot end this chapter without sharing one valuable lesson I learned, from a lad we'll call Simon, who had been placed at BBR for several weeks that summer by Canadian Social Services.

Simon was in my cabin group for about 3 weeks and this was not easy for either of us. He did not want to be there and he was not going to hide that from anyone. He consistently failed to show up for activities, remained silent and sullen through camp fire each evening and would not participate at all in our cabin discussions.

When I tried to talk to him about it, he looked at the ground and told me he was only there because no one else wanted him around. They certainly did not want him at home. That is why he had been placed at Birch Bay for as long as we would take him. I tried everything to encourage him and cheer him up, but all to no avail. Simon did not want to know. He did not want to be there. In fact, he told me, he didn't really want to be anywhere.

We were about half way through his third week and he only had about 3 days left before he was due to be sent on to a new foster family, when Simon one morning seemed to come alive. He appeared to be released from all the heaviness that had weighed him down and he suddenly had a voracious appetite for life, for fun and for making the most of the day. Where he had not been showing up for activities, we were amazed that he was first to arrive. At the camp fire, when for the previous 2 weeks he had just sat there looking at his feet, he suddenly started volunteering to take part in every skit or game and singing as loud as anyone in all of the songs.

It was in our cabin discussion that evening that I realised this lad had really made some massive leap forward in his own self-esteem, confidence and appetite for life. He had also grasped a profound insight which I realised I could learn from too.

It was Thursday evening and the kids were staying until the Saturday. With 2 days to go, I felt it was important to talk about going home. What had we learned? What would be different as a result of our shared week together?

When on this particular evening I broached the subject, asking how the kids felt about going back to the real world after such a fun week together, none of us could believe it when Simon spoke up immediately.

'I don't see it like that,' he said. Every eye turned towards a boy who had been pretty well silent for 18 days.

'What do you mean?' I said. 'After all, you guys are all heading home the day after tomorrow.'

'I know,' he continued, 'but to me the real world is what we have shared here this week. We are now all just going back to the mess that man is making of the world we live in!'

It was humbling to see Simon's change of perspective that had been sparked as a result of his stay at Birch Bay Ranch, and it was reassuring to know that BBR would be there for him each year for subsequent summers as he was growing up.

4.

The Canadian Rockies

Two other incidents which occurred towards the end of the summer were particularly formative in the years to come, when we eventually embraced the challenge of setting up a similar youth adventure outreach in the UK. They were Adventure Camp and a road trip across the Rockies to Vancouver.

As the weeks went by, I was aware that the leaders were getting progressively more tired. This was no doubt the result of several weeks of back to back camps, with one group of children leaving late on Saturday morning and the next batch of excited campers arriving Sunday afternoon, so there was no clear day off in the course of the summer.

But as August wore on Tessa and I detected a growing excitement about Adventure Camp. This was a unique week in the year when canoes, climbing and hiking gear, tents and cooking kit were loaded onto trailers and into vans and a group of older campers was invited to join the team for a week in the Canadian Rockies. I was amazed at the level of detailed preparation required in the days leading up to our departure to ensure everyone was properly equipped for the different activities we would be providing, and of course, well fed.

As we headed off in the Birch Bay Ranch minibuses to our camp site above Rocky Mountain House, there was a real sense of anticipation. For the young people who had enjoyed summers at BBR since they were 7 or 8, this long-awaited event would mark a turning point, an opportunity to put all the skills in climbing and canoeing they had learned in previous years to good use, but now in much more adventurous terrain. It also marked a transition between coming as a camper to BBR and being invited back as a leader the following year.

When we finally arrived at our camp site, the evening was warm and dry and we laid our sleeping bags out under the stars and slept. I was woken by the smell of coffee and bacon frying over an open fire. That morning we breakfasted with the foothills of the Rocky Mountains as our majestic backdrop.

It was day one of Adventure Camp and we headed off to a local crag for our first taste of climbing on real rock. Up to this time, the artificial climbing walls at Birch Bay Ranch had marked the extent of my climbing experience so it was great to get out onto the real thing, and in such an amazing setting! The exercise of finding footholds and handholds in the natural rock, and making them work, was so much more satisfying than the more obvious progress up the series of brightly coloured resin holds and wooden blocks on the climbing walls at the ranch, and the mountain setting made it all the more memorable.

I will always remember the experience of emerging at the top of the route, having started from a floor cushioned by a thick bed of pine needles in the steeply inclining forest. The air was perfumed by the fresh scent of trees such as aspen, white spruce and lodgepole pine. This aroma grew imperceptibly stronger as the sun climbed higher above our side of the valley. As I 'topped out' and began to relax a little, I turned to see the vista of the whole valley spread below us. An impressive expanse of woodland, punctuated by rocky outcrops, sweeping down to the evident, but hidden path of a river deep in the valley below. This bigger picture which had been totally obscured by the trees at the base of the climb was somehow brought into sharper reality by the clear mountain air, laced with forest aromas wafted up from below, on the freshening breeze.

What a fantastic start to our adventure week in the Canadian Rockies. On a more sobering note, I also learned that day, first hand, the importance of wearing a helmet in a rocky environment, especially where people are moving around directly above. As the instructors were setting up the climb at the top and we were at the base sorting out ropes and gear, I had taken a moment to look up to see if I could work out a route up the crag above, trying to visualise the holds I would use. Suddenly a loud pistol crack close to my right temple jolted me from my musings. A stone no larger than a golf ball had been dislodged above and fallen straight down, catching the edge of my helmet, and away. No harm done, other than a slight indentation in the fibreglass. If I had not been wearing that helmet . . . who knows?

Trail Mix, Bear Bells and an Indian Sauna

Next on the agenda was a hiking trip. As we packed our rucksacks for the 2-day walk on some of the extensive mountain trails in the Canadian Rockies, there was a lot of talk about two features in particular, both of which were new to me: trail mix and bear bells.

Trail mix is a fantastic invention. A mix of high energy tasty snacks is thrown into a bag to give a good balance of quick release and more sustained energy food, which is delicious. The great news is that there is no right, or wrong, recipe. You put in what you think will keep you going when the going gets tough. On that trip we were provided with a bag of Trail mix: a wonderful concoction of granola, M&Ms, mini marshmallows, cashew nuts and dried fruit. What an incentive to keep going when we started to feel drained! I am forever grateful to the team at Birch Bay for introducing me to this wonderful excuse to eat whatever I like, thrown together in an extravagantly high-energy mix, and always with the plausible reasoning that when I am out hiking or biking, I need to keep my energy levels up – brilliant!

Bear bells were less appetising but seemed like a very good idea when they were explained to me. They work on the principle that bears are not naturally aggressive, but it is best not to surprise one – be it black, brown or grisly – by stumbling on it unawares. Attached to the outside of our back packs, brightly coloured little bells jingled as we walked along, giving any bears ahead of us down the path plenty of warning of our approach and time, perhaps sadly, to disappear into the undergrowth and avoid unexpected confrontation.

At last we arrived at the planned camp site at the end of the first day, a clearing in the woods, beside a small river. Some of us rested whilst others helped build a fire and prepare the evening meal. After dinner we were instructed to pack most of our luggage, including any food and especially our toothpaste, into our bag and suspend it from trees some distance from where we were sleeping. Like the bear bells, this was to avoid any unplanned visits from bears attracted by the smell of food or the mint in our toothpaste.

As we were getting this organised, I was very aware that the mountain air temperature was falling rapidly. What an unexpected bonus then, especially for those who had developed aches and pains after a full days hiking, when our leaders announced they were building a Native American sauna. I hadn't noticed but they had surrounded our cooking fire with a number of rocks which had been heating effectively during dinner. A large tarp had been draped from a tree to create a tipi-shaped shelter. I was asked to help bring the heated rocks to the tipi, using a small shovel.

We were then invited into the tipi as water from the river was poured onto the hot rocks. Before we knew it we found ourselves, in the middle of nowhere, enjoying a very effective, warming and soothing sauna – before retiring to our sleeping bags for the night.

Canadian Canoeing

The 2-day hiking trip was followed by 2 days of canoeing on the Saskatchewan River, taking us back east towards Edmonton and home. This fantastic river provided a rich mix of clear, flat water flowing through beautiful foothills, interspaced with some really fun roller coaster rapids. Neither Tessa nor I had done any canoeing in moving water before so this was a new experience.

Our aluminium Grumman canoes were tough and reasonably light and I was amazed how easy it was to repair my boat, after I'd reshaped it round a large boulder in the middle of the river, bending it backwards. When we eventually got it to the side and hauled it up onto the riverbank, both ends, which were normally raised slightly off the ground by the curve of the boat, dug into the sand leaving a sharply defined triangular gap under the middle of the boat and a gash about six inches long. This was not ideal, especially as we still had a day and a half left to paddle, with our luggage. Unperturbed, the river leaders jumped up and down on the middle of the boat until it was more or less the right shape again and sealed the crack with a good length of duct tape, which stuck surprisingly well to the aluminium hull; a repair that would not have been so easy on our more modern plastic boats.

'Ferry Tale' Romance

With adventure camp behind us, our summer at Birch Bay Ranch was drawing to a close, but we still had one more adventure to look forward to. One of the Canadians on our team in Sudan had been in touch when he heard we were over in Alberta. He was planning a road trip across the Rockies, from Edmonton to Vancouver, to visit a mutual friend, a nurse who had also been in Sudan and was now living on the west coast. Would we like to go along with him? What an opportunity!

We were thankful to get permission from the Camp Director at BBR to take a week off before heading back to the UK and were able to take up the offer. The drive back up into the Rockies soon took us beyond the area we'd visited on Adventure Camp, and into Banff National Park. We camped each night, this time with tents, which was no bad thing as autumn was definitely starting to set in and the nights were cold.

For Tessa and me it was good to get time away from the camp environment, especially as I had probably taken a little too seriously the 'no dating rule' at BBR. Early on the second morning of our trip I went for a walk along the shores of the lake we had camped beside, and met Tessa armed with an axe, chopping wood for our early morning fire. None of the precautions I'd learned for safety in the mountains prepared me for this encounter. Bear bells and placing food a safe distance from our sleeping area were all to no avail as we chatted. The kiss we shared beside the lake that morning was to prove far more dangerous to my peace of mind than I could have imagined. As the journey across the Rockies progressed into the beauty of the Okanagan Valley and down towards the Pacific, I knew there was one important life adventure I could shy away from no longer.

We had engaged in a long distance relationship that had spanned the past eight years since we'd both left Kingsbury High School in North London. Tessa had lived as an au pair in Brussels, then on to University in Bournemouth before teaching English for a year in the French city of Le Mans. Meanwhile I had been nursing in Whitechapel and living for a year in Sudan. I knew that the long years of waiting were finally over.

As we approached the beautiful city of Vancouver, I realised that I would never have another friend like this, or a more stunning bride. There was also unlikely to be a more romantic place for a proposal, especially as the ferry from Vancouver to Vancouver Island took us onto the Pacific Ocean. So it was with a real sense of anticipation and dread excitement that I boarded the ferry to Victoria. I was very aware that once I popped the question there could be no going back. If she said 'yes', there would be the stark realisation that we were about to walk into a life-changing situation that could never be reversed. This natural caution was no match for the stunning prize and the promise of such a lovely lifelong friend.

Having said that, I was young and this was scary. I am ashamed to admit I had to set myself a deadline. If I was going to ask Tessa at all, I had to seize the moment and make it happen on this ferry, in the beauty of this Pacific sunshine. We boarded the ferry to Vancouver Island, our hosts so proud to be showing their English guests this jewel in the beautiful city of Vancouver. As we sailed out into the shimmering natural harbour, with clear blue sky above and the magnificent backdrop of the Rocky Mountains behind, my friends noticed that I seemed to become strangely distant. We had all just settled ourselves on the warm deck to enjoy the wonderful view and our picnic of smoked salmon bagels when, I am told, I just got up and went for a walk around the ferry, on my own.

What on earth Tessa and our two Canadian friends must have thought of me I don't want to imagine but I was genuinely struggling with the momentous task ahead. So much so that when we got off the ferry in Victoria I had failed miserably to pluck up the courage to ask this beautiful girl to marry me.

I'm afraid I can hardly remember our brief stay in the renowned tourist location of Victoria, apart from a building that reminded me of London's Harrods and a brief coastal walk, looking out at the Pacific Ocean stretching west to the horizon. I could hardly think about anything other than that return ferry journey the next day. I was going to ask Tessa to marry me, and I was going to do it today. Help!

As we boarded the ferry back to Vancouver I was even more immersed in my own world than on the way out. No sooner had we settled down again on the sun drenched deck for another picnic, than I grabbed Tessa's hand and asked if she wanted to walk round the deck of the boat. We soon found a moment with no one else around and stood looking at the wonderful view of Vancouver. There was the bridge, the myriad of small boats and planes going this way and that, all framed for us by that ever present Rocky Mountain backdrop.

This was it; now or never. 'So . . . will you marry me?' I blurted out with no preamble at all. Timing, they say, is everything. The moment I chose for this life-changing question was also the moment just after Tessa had taken a large bite of bagel. The question prompted a sharp intake of breath, peppered with smoked salmon and mayonnaise, which of course resulted not in the romantic dreamy-eyed reply I'd been hoping for, but rather a near Heimlich-worthy paroxysm of choking and coughing, as Tessa fought desperately to clear her airway.

As I waited for an answer a number of concerned passengers gathered round us. I half-heartedly offered to pat her on the back, but eventually the coughing subsided. Tessa's reply, when it came, was not entirely what I wanted to hear, or expected.

'Are you being serious?' She asked, a fair question on reflection, given that I had kept her waiting on and off for eight years, in a relationship that had spanned three continents.

When I said, 'of course I'm serious,' she threw the rest of the bagel overboard and her arms around me in one fluid movement and the rest is history.

Men and Boys!

The return journey to Edmonton passed in a bit of a dream and it was not long before we were packing bags and saying our goodbyes before heading back to London for preparations for a wedding and the second year at Kings.

So our first foray into adventure youth work ended. We had both been impressed by the transformation brought about by just one week at Birch Bay Ranch in the lives of hundreds of children and teenagers that summer. We felt sure that the mix of fun, friendship and exciting activities, all in such a positive Christian atmosphere, where each child was clearly highly valued, had given us a model which we were to try to emulate back in the UK. We will always be grateful to the staff team at Birch Bay for making us so welcome and giving us such a great insight into their superb youth ministry.

We had one stop to make on our way back to Heathrow however. We could not fly back to the UK without calling in to visit a wonderful couple living near Toronto who had been very special to me during my time in Sudan.

Before heading out to Khartoum, there had been a two month training course at the headquarters of Emmanuel International in Ontario. Jim and Joan were volunteers at

EI. They had children of a similar age to me and had really welcomed me into their family during my stay. It almost felt like they had adopted me as their British son whilst in Canada. They had even flown out to Damazin from Toronto for a few weeks to help with some construction whilst I was out there. When they heard I was in Canada and was now planning to get married they pretty much insisted that we drop down to Toronto on the way back so they could meet my bride to be, and for Jim to share some 'father-son wisdom' with me on the subject of marriage.

Jim is a man with many hats. Amongst other things he is an accomplished hunter and an expert on firearms. He is one of the few people licensed to cull rogue bears which occasionally become a danger to isolated homesteads in rural Ontario.

Whilst we were staying with them, Jim got a call to head north as a bear had started worrying local livestock and threatening a small rural community. This was the perfect opportunity for us to get some man to man time together and for Joan to get to know Tessa better back at home.

I have to admit I was a little intrigued about this adoptive 'father-son' bonding expedition, as we climbed into his Toyota Hilux, with three hounds in the pick-up and a rack of rifles behind us in the cab. It was certainly a new experience for a suburban lad from North London to be driven out into the Canadian wilderness in search of a rogue bear.

We'd been driving for about three hours, chatting about this and that, when he suddenly became more serious. He turned his bearded face towards me whilst he was driving, and fixed me, particularly with his right eye, which seemed more prominent somehow than the left.

'Now Listen Jaarn,' he said in his ponderous Canadian drawl, 'you'll be gett'n married soon.'

'Yes Jim, that's the plan.'

'Well I want you to remember this and don't you forget it . . .'

I was all ears for the wisdom that was to follow: 'Always remember that when a gurl grows up, she becomes a woman . . .'

What? Is that it? Is this what I had flown 4 hours and driven all this way to hear?

'But,' he continued, 'when a boy grows up, he just becomes a bigger boy!'

I looked round me in the cab of his 4x4, at the rack of guns secured behind us, and I couldn't argue. We never did find that bear. But I found some great wisdom. I am not exactly sure how Jim's observation about the sexes has helped us in our marriage since, but his insight certainly has a ring of truth about it.

By the time we got back to their home it was time to pack and move on once again, this time for London and home. We returned encouraged and challenged by all that we had learned, convinced that what we had seen during our summer at Birch Bay Ranch had given us the blueprint for an outreach to young people in the UK, through adventure and education – and *the serious business of having fun!*

5.

A Club, a Commitment, a Community

Two immediate projects loomed large as soon as we arrived back in London. The first involved gaining experience in youth work and the second the small matter of organising a wedding and finding a place to live. That meant going to see two very significant people: Tessa's father, to ask for Tessa's hand in marriage, and the vicar of our church, the Reverend Richard Bewes, to ask about youth work, and of course the availability of the church on Saturdays in December.

I was certainly more nervous about speaking to Tessa's father. It was, after all, a big question. What if he should say no? In the event he graciously said that he was wondering when I would get around to it and asked if I was sure I knew what I was letting myself in for. Finally he asked if, seeing as I am 6'4", I'd change the light bulb in his study. If I was going to be part of the family I might as well start to make myself useful straight away!

With his approval, the project was on. We planned to set the date for Saturday 12 December, just three months away, so we had our work cut out. And then we'd need to find somewhere to live.

Richard, having referred us to the administrator for church availability, was intrigued by our calling to youth work, particularly as he pointed out that there was not very much youth work in our church at the time. All Souls Langham Place is a city church positioned at the north end of Regent Street right in the heart of London's West End. Renowned for excellent teaching and with a strong music tradition, Tessa and I, along with hundreds of other students, had both greatly benefitted from our involvement there. However, although All Souls back in the 1980s had a great student life, and the congregation had a strong contingent of young professionals, there were not so many families and young people in the congregation at that time. It did begin to grow significantly over the next few years, with a healthy influx of both families and young people, but Richard was right to point out that it was perhaps not then the best place to assist with and 'learn' youth work.

He did make a very perceptive and constructive suggestion, however. Why didn't we visit the Clubhouse that following Sunday and see if we might want to get involved there? 'Club' was the community centre established by John Stott, while he had been Rector of All Souls, to serve the community of Fitzrovia, within the parish of All Souls. In addition to a couple of Sunday services which took place in the small sports hall, it also had a vibrant youth work for young people drawn mainly from two largish council estates, one on either side of the Euston Road. There were various clubs for different age groups on most nights of the week.

It didn't take us long to get fully involved in the congregation and youth work at the Clubhouse and this proved to be an excellent training ground to learn more about working with young people and urban youth culture.

At about the same time I got back in touch with Graham Harris, a good friend from school days, who had had the dubious pleasure of sitting next to me for several years in the trombone section of Brent Youth Symphony Orchestra. Since I'd last seen him, Graham had been away at Birmingham University where he had immersed himself in the climbing and kayaking clubs, alongside his occasional forays into maths and statistics.

When he heard about our summer at BBR and our plans to try to establish something similar here in the UK, he offered to take me paddling and climbing, to teach me the basics. Much of this early training took place just down the road at the 'Y', the YMCA centre in Tottenham Court Road, which conveniently had a pool with kayaks and a climbing wall.

It is amazing now to look back at the ways in which so much was falling into place to prepare us for our own big adventure. These were in many ways foundational years for what was to become Adventure*Plus*.

Home and Away

A more urgent need was to find a place where Tessa and I would be able to live after our wedding, now just two months away. Clearly it was not going to work for her to move in with me and Stewart the Australian chef and the rest of the Aussies, Kiwis and Americans in Parliament Hill.

About this time I met a student who was due to move out of her one bedroom flat in Lambeth, just south of the

Thames, and she wondered if I would like the flat for Tessa and myself. 'Result' or 'a real God-send' or both?! It certainly was exactly what we needed and the timing was perfect. Plus it was affordable, even for two students, me in the second year of an Environmental Sciences degree and Tessa studying for her Law Society Finals. It was not without a twinge of sadness that I edited myself out of that '*Neighbours* set' in Hampstead to secure the flat for Tessa and myself.

Get Me to the Church on Time!

The all-consuming backdrop to all these changes was of course the small matter of a wedding to sort out, with very limited funds and the challenges of our two courses, which were both demanding for very different reasons: Tessa's because Law Society finals are very easy not to pass, and mine because I was still battling with my total lack of background in the sciences.

This was not helped by the fact that we had not left ourselves very much time. We were now well into October and we had managed to book the church for mid-December which was in itself quite an achievement. Positioned where it is, All Souls is in great demand for all kinds of events, especially in the run up to Christmas, and we were very grateful to Richard Bewes for allowing us to get married there. We were also delighted when he agreed to conduct the service himself – a great privilege which meant so much to us both.

I am sure there were quite a number of people wondering why we had set such a tight target for a wedding date, especially as we had been an item for at least eight years by now, and I certainly had shown no particular eagerness to tie the knot before we had spent the summer together in Canada! The real reason for the ambitious time scale was that plans were already being hatched to work with a Ghanaian orphanage the following summer and to write my final year thesis whilst out there, pursuing my continued interest in sub-Saharan community development. It was clear that we would only be able to travel and stay together whilst in Ghana if we were married. The other obvious and less immediate choice for a wedding date would have been the following Easter, but neither of us wanted the pressure of end of year exams looming so large right after our wedding. Imminent exams are not the best backdrop to a honeymoon.

Amazingly all the plans fell into place wonderfully well. We even inherited beautiful flowers from the wedding which preceded ours in the church! I had written a wedding fanfare for Tessa, for brass quartet. We were so privileged to be joined by a number of friends from the All Souls Orchestra to add another touch of real quality to that special day, and by Lis Hobden, our favourite soloist, whose rendition of 'Such is the Mystery' by Sir Cliff Richard, was just beautiful.

The only slight element of comic confusion on the day itself stemmed from a phone call I received on my wedding morning. The trombone player who had kindly agreed to play, including a key part in the wedding fanfare, called to say it was his mother's birthday so he was up in the Wirral visiting her! That was the bad news. The good news was that at least it was the trombone player, so I could fill in for his part. I hastily made arrangements to borrow a trombone and I played in the wedding fanfare, which was set in the programme as a triumphal exit from the signing of the register. Unfortunately that meant I had to sneak out from the signing without Tessa. I noted one or two quizzical looks amongst friends and family on both sides of the church as Tessa then emerged, accompanied by a splendid Wedding Fanfare, on the arm of the best man, my brother!

Youth and Community

We returned from honeymoon to start married life together in our new flat in Lambeth shortly after New Year 1988. Along with our studies, life at Club continued to educate and absorb us. We enjoyed getting involved in two youth clubs for different age groups and learned lots, both from the young people and the leaders.

Based in the community of Fitzrovia, in London's fashionable postcode of W1, and surrounded by the iconic West End addresses of Regent Street, Oxford Street, Tottenham Court Road and Marylebone Road, visitors are often surprised to find such a strong sense of community amid the head offices of well-known IT, engineering and fashion companies. In fact the area is also home to thousands of local people, many living on a good-sized council estate in the neighbourhood, and in rented flats.

The Clubhouse was, and still is, a fantastic resource, a meeting place for local people providing a heart of welcome and support in that unique community. Youth clubs for different age groups were provided most evenings of the week. Regular activities included pool or snooker, football in the sports hall, band practices or sitting chatting and listening to music. And it was not just a youth centre; there was also a thriving day care centre for the elderly, several other local support networks and of course a growing church congregation.

As Tessa and I got more involved over a number of weeks, it was good to get to know the young people and other youth volunteers better. Two or three times each week we would buzz over the River Thames on our small motorbike from our flat in Lambeth. I had to chuckle at the comment from one of the young lads at the end of a Club night as we climbed on our Kawasaki GPZ 305, to head home.

'Where are you going?'

'Back home.'

'Where's that?'

'Lambeth.'

'Lambeth? South of the River? Hope you've got your passport. That's not London, that's France!'

It wasn't long before an opportunity arose to move into a flat linked to the Clubhouse in Grafton Mews, only a five-minute walk away. This meant we could get more involved in Club life and would see the young people we were working with on a more regular basis, often bumping into them at the shops or when out in the local area. After a few months, having got to know the young people better, we both began to be excited by the idea of offering a forum where, in addition to providing general youth club activities, there would be a chance to explore some challenging life-questions with Club members. We discussed this with the rest of the youth team and decided to offer to put on an alternative programme called 'Club with a Difference'.

We would meet weekly on Thursdays, the only evening that the Clubhouse was not already being used. On alternate

weeks the young people could pick any subject they wanted
to talk about and that would be the theme for the evening.
We would all respect each other enough to share honestly and
openly our views on the subject and explore the implications
for our friends and families or for the wider community. It was
no secret that Tessa and I would bring our Christian perspective to the discussions. That, after all, was our viewpoint. It
was also clear that others would be sharing from their different
opinions. Every second week we would all go out on a trip in
the Clubhouse minibus to another part of London.

Some of the other youth leaders at the time were enthusiastic about the idea whilst others thought that the young
people would never go for it: 'Why would a group of young
people want to think about questions like these or discuss
God-related issues?'

Reservations like these were not always easy to answer but
since the teen years are a time of adjusting and growing up in
so many areas of life, we felt it was wrong to assume young
people would *not* want to explore important and challenging
issues.

Tessa and I had been greatly encouraged during our time
at Birch Bay Ranch to be confident about our faith. While we
didn't have all the answers, we had a definite sense that this
was the right thing to be doing.

Club with a Difference

A date was set for our first Club with a Difference and Tessa
and I arrived on the day to set up with two other helpers.
When the selection of tasty 'munchies' and hot drinks had

been prepared, there was nothing left to do but sit and wait to see if any of the young people who'd said they were interested would actually show up.

6.45 p.m. was the advertised start time. Our aim for that first week was to meet and chat around the whole idea and see what the young people thought and, if they liked the sound of it, what themes they might like us to tackle, so we could plan in advance some material for our first few sessions.

When 7 p.m. came and went and we had no takers we were preparing to pack up and head home when we heard voices outside and about seven young people arrived to see what this was all about. We were really encouraged by their enthusiasm for both parts of the plan – the outings and the themed weeks exploring their chosen issues.

In the weeks that followed, a consistent group of regulars became the core of Club with a Difference, both for the trips out and the discussion weeks. As the process unfolded, it became clear to us that adults should never presume that young people would not want to explore those bigger life questions. Young people are often hungry to talk about things that perhaps both our society in general and the education system in particular ignore or devalue.

Our fortnightly trips out were also highlights for us all. Destinations included a trip to Camden Lock, then on to my old haunts of Hampstead Heath for an evening of general 'out there' fun and frisbee, and a visit to the South Bank. The sense of space on the Heath and by the River Thames offered a refreshing change from the crowded streets of Fitzrovia, where we all spent so much of our everyday lives.

Another key lesson that has stayed with me ever since was a growing awareness of how perceptive young people are. This was the era of Guns N' Roses and Motorhead, which of course affected the music that was constantly playing at Club and the dress code of many of the young people.

Whilst Tessa at least had long hair, I would never pass for a heavy rocker and decided not to try to be something I was not. We were encouraged that our decision not to try to dress or act like them did not seem to present a barrier. This was strengthened one evening during our discussion time when someone commented that they liked us because they felt they knew who we were, because we were not trying to be something we were not. The fact that we knew who we were and were not about to try to change it to fit in better seemed to provide a sound basis on which to build genuine relationships and mutual trust.

As the weeks rolled on, real friendships began to develop between the youth leaders and the young people. Tessa and I felt privileged to get to know this group of young people at a more relaxed yet deeper level. The members of Club with a Difference looked forward to Club nights and soon developed the habit of coming to knock on the window of our ground floor flat, often more than an hour before we were due to open up at the Clubhouse, to ask if were coming out. The answer was always positive, but 'not until quarter to. See you there!'

6.

'Champions'

After a couple of months we felt, along with the other volunteer leaders who were helping us, that it might be good to work on a project with the group which would give them a chance to make a real contribution, in relation to the material we were discussing. Something they could get their teeth into. Tessa and I recalled one of the skits which was always so popular, and powerful, from the camp fires at Birch Bay Ranch. It was a drama acted out to a song by Carman, a Christian rock musician popular in North America at the time.

The idea could work well in this setting for a number of reasons. The soundtrack was powerful and well engineered. It had a heavy rock feel which we thought the young people would feel at home with, and we could see how the graphic lyrics, describing the war between good and evil as a street fight between Satan and Jesus, could be staged as a powerful performance within the Clubhouse setting.

One Club night, after our themed discussion, we raised the idea with the group and played them the track, which was called 'The Champion'. It appeared that everyone liked the song itself and most liked the idea of doing a drama, but the prospect of presenting it to their mates and other club members was more challenging. For some this would push them right to the edge of their comfort zone and for others it would take them beyond it. So what should we do? Was there a way forward or was this all going a little too far, in terms of commitment to a project and in dealing with a spiritual issue, the fight between good and evil? In the end we decided we would all think about it and come back to the next meeting with a decision.

When we next met there had clearly been quite a bit of discussion and the decision was to go with the challenge of working this up as a drama, and then, if we liked how things were shaping up, we would consider putting it on as a performance for other club members, youth leaders, parents and friends.

Plans for the following couple of months centred round pulling together what was, as far as we knew, the first performance in the UK of *The Champion*. We agreed roles and two local young lads took the parts of Jesus and Satan, with their mates making up the opposing forces of angels and demons. As we started to rehearse, the plan was that the soundtrack would play clear and loud, the main characters miming a closely choreographed interpretation of the music, mouthing the words of their characters as the track played.

As the weeks went on it was great to see a growing momentum of energy and enthusiasm for this project. Characters learned their words and a plan came together, with creative input from the young people, for a graphic and effective stage set. We decided we could get maximum effect if we performed it at night, in a blacked out hall, so the only light was from the spots that we'd managed to acquire locally. Our only prop was to be a simple scaffold tower plus, if we could get it, some dry ice, to add a touch of mystery and a sense of the unexpected at the start of the performance. Confidence was growing in the group and at the end of one evening's rehearsal we broached the question of whether they wanted us to book the Clubhouse and put out publicity for an open performance. Most were keen to make it happen and the group decided to go for it.

We set a date for a month in advance, booked the hall and designed and put up posters. We were committed. As the days started to tick by we were very aware that a number of others involved in youth work at Club were interested to see if this event was actually going to happen. It was not uncommon when planning an event demanding commitment that the young people might not follow the plan through to the end, or perhaps a group might simply just not turn up on the day.

On the positive side, rehearsals were going well and there was a growing sense of excitement as the young people could begin to see the plan coming together and visualise a hard-hitting and effective performance that they would be proud to be a part of. We also had fantastic support from a number of members of the youth team at Club and I was encouraged and delighted by the surprising can-do response of the stage manager from the New London Theatre, just a mile down the road.

I had called and explained that we were working to put on a drama with a group of young people at a local community centre and that we planned to use dry ice for effect at the start of the production, but that it was not easy for us to access the small quantity we would need. Was there any chance we might come down and 'borrow' some from his theatre?

The guy on the other end of the phone could not have been more positive and generous. He asked a bit more detail about the kind of thing we had in mind and when we were planning to perform it. I was lost for words when he asked what kind of smoke machine we had!

'Oh . . .'

I was grateful when he interrupted the embarrassed silence. 'In that case you're also going to need two metal buckets, a kettle and some leather gloves.'

We arranged that I would bike down on the evening of the performance with one of our young people to collect the frozen blocks. He advised that we would definitely need leather gloves and that we should be able to transport them in the lined back box of my motorcycle.

Everything seemed to be moving in the right direction until 2 days before the performance, when we had what was supposed to be a full run-through. It did not go well. Folks arrived late and when they did show up it became clear that a couple of the key characters had not learned their words, and there were only 2 days to go! The effect of this on the rest of the cast was clear as they realised that if the performance was not as good as we had persuaded them it could be they would be seriously embarrassed in front of their mates.

Reading between the lines, it was clear that there had been a steady build-up of peer pressure from members of the club and other friends who were not involved in the production. Our team members were determined not to make fools of themselves, or embarrass their mates, especially as we had just heard that a group from another estate was expected to turn up to watch the show. The evening ended with half of the guys saying they were not going to do it! Oh, help!

As they left us to clear up after the disastrous rehearsal, we felt pretty desperate about the situation but decided it would be good to pray for the whole process, that the young people would have the courage to surmount the increasing pressures around them and that it would result in a positive experience for all and a real confidence boost for the cast who had had the guts to put their heads above the parapet of peer pressure, even to get this far.

We were due to meet as a full cast for the final run-through the next evening, which was the evening before the show. I spent the afternoon putting up the scaffold tower with a couple of the guys involved in the production, but the word from them was not good. They had heard that about half of the cast was not planning to show up that night for our final run-through, or for the performance.

One thing was certain, however: if we didn't have the scaffolding up, the show could definitely not go ahead, even if they did decide to turn up. So we just kept working to put everything in place and I for one was praying that it would all come together. When we had finished it looked great. As it grew dark we tried the spots, and we could immediately see what a dramatic stark visual impact the stage set would make, if only the guys would stay with the plan.

When the time came for our final run-through, about half of the cast arrived ready to get started, but they were in no mood to hang around if the show was going nowhere. After about 40 minutes of waiting and rehearsing their parts, those that had appeared were getting ready to walk away. We were losing our grip and the whole project was about to fall apart.

It was just at this point that the guys who had been helping with the scaffolding during the afternoon reappeared with the other lads who had said they were not going to go through with the performance. Were they up for it now? They said they'd give it a go this evening and see how it went.

With the scaffolding and lighting in place we began the run-through, in pitch black. Out of the silence the music started, a mysterious, almost spooky synthesised introduction playing into the darkness, setting the scene for the deep, reverberating voice of Carman:

> In the vast expanse of a timeless place,
> Where silence ruled the outer space,
> Ominously towering, it stood,
> The symbol of a spirit war
> Between the one named Lucifer,
> And the Morning Star, the ultimate of good.

Everything was coming together as we'd hoped and you could feel the confidence surging through the team as each person prepared for their role in our production of *The Champion*. Still the mysterious music continued:

> Enveloped by a trillion planets,
> Clean as lightning and hard as granite,
> A cosmic coliseum would host the end
> Of the war between the lord of sin and death,
> And the Omnipotent Creator of man's first breath.

Bright, clinical, white light from our four spots pierced the blackness right on cue – the lads on lighting were playing their part to perfection.

The tempo picked up in the track as a heavy rock beat was hammered out by the drums. As the song played through, the cast each came in as rehearsed and the growing confidence and team spirit was almost palpable as these young lads and girls started to believe in themselves and what we could achieve together – even in front of their mates. As the stage fight between the forces of good and evil reached their climax, with the apparent defeat of the Son of God, the history-changing twist came at the end of the 'ten count' of apparent defeat.

We knew that this was going to be a memorable and brilliant performance and a significant achievement for each of the young people who had volunteered to take part. So, with some final words of encouragement, and a reminder to refine one or two key lines, we parted and I arranged to meet Richie, one of our technical helpers, at Club about an hour before the performance the next day. He'd agreed to come down with me to the New London Theatre to collect the dry ice.

What we still did not know, however, was if anyone would show up to see this performance which had absorbed so much of our time and energies over the past couple of months.

Lights, Darkness, Action

Richie and I left the bike by the stage door of The New London Theatre as instructed, walked in off the street and asked the surprised porter for the stage manager. Knowing we were on a tight schedule he came straight down to meet us and took us in a lift to the back of the stage. He explained we needed to be quiet as the performance of *Cats* was already under way.

'Is the young lady helping with the production?' he asked, looking at Richie, my young, clean shaven assistant and Guns N' Roses fan! I caught his eye and we each suppressed a laugh as we came out of the lift.

I was amazed to find that we were actually walking, hunched low, right under the stage during the performance. The thin panels above us were creaking and bending as we heard, and almost felt, the dancers prowling and leaping around just a few inches above our heads. We each pulled on the leather gloves so the blocks did not stick to our hands, and loaded about six of the icy blocks into our lined holdall, before saying a huge 'Thank you' and heading for the lift and the stage door.

Soon we were back on the street and loading our frozen cargo carefully into our pre-lined back box, for our unique courier ride back to Cleveland Street and our own performance. When we got back to the Clubhouse, Tessa and the rest of the crew were getting themselves and everything else in place for the start. Uppermost in my mind, apart from setting up the dry-ice machine, which consisted of two metal buckets and two urns of boiling water, was the question that had been haunting me all day. Would anyone show up? We had to wait until just before the performance before we could go on stage with the dry ice – or we would ruin the element of surprise.

With 2 minutes to go all the lights went off and it was suddenly utterly dark. As we sneaked in to position the dry ice, it was evident that the hall was absolutely full. I tried to sneak past the front row to get to my position, over and above the heckling that was coming from the crowd, all seated by now in the darkness. I was aware of at least a couple of people spitting into the area in front of the crowd where we were now walking. But at least they had showed up and in fantastic numbers.

This was it. Would the idea, borrowed from a camp fire in Birch Bay Ranch, Alberta, work here in an inner city youth club in Central London? We were about to find out.

As the heckling continued in the darkness, we lowered the first two blocks of dry ice into the metal bins on either side of the stage and poured on the boiling water. The loud hiss, as the hot water hit the frozen blocks, surprised me and stunned the crowd into a sudden silence of expectation.

Glancing chords broke the silence and gave way to the first eerie theme tune of Carman's *The Champion*. We were on. This was it! And we were playing to a full house!

> The crowd was silent.
> It was still pitch black.
> In the vast expanse of a timeless place,
> Where silence ruled the outer space,
> Ominously towering, it stood . . .

The cue 'spotlight to scaffold' created a sharp linear shadow against the familiar Clubhouse mural. Steam from the dry ice stole across the floor, enveloping the base of the scaffold tower, swirling in shadow against the wall, in the circle of light picked out by the spot. The crowd was still silent. Expectant.

Enveloped by a trillion planets,
Clean as lightning and hard as granite,
A cosmic coliseum would host the end
Of the war between the lord of sin and death,
And the Omnipotent Creator of man's first breath . . .
Who will decide who forever will be the Champion.

The drum beat kicks in. Synthesizer and guitars pick up the tempo:

The audience for the 'Fight of the Ages'
was assembled and in place.
The angels came in splendour from a star.
The saints that had gone before were there:
Jeremiah, Enoch, Job.
They were singing the 'Song of Zion'
on David's harp.

The demons arrived, offensive and vile,
cursing and blaspheming God.
Followed by their 'trophies' dead and gone . . .

As the young people came on stage in their two groups, representing good and evil, the stage was set for our own drama to play out. There was no doubt that the audience who had started out ready to heckle and have a laugh were now 100 per cent with us.

The performance rolled on – all 8 minutes, 34 seconds of it – building to the culmination of the battle, and the ten count of defeat, in the fight arena, as Jesus is lying beaten up

on the floor with God the Father as judge, counting down to
the last five . . .

'Four . . .

Three . . .

Two . . .'

'*Won – he has won!*'

Jesus recovers from the final blow, bursting through the
death which could not hold him. As the music played to its
conclusion, applause from the crowd replaced the recorded
music and the hall lights went up for the first time that night.
The guys took a well-deserved bow in front of their mates.

Lessons Learned

We had all learned much from working so closely together.
Of the many lessons I took away from that time at the
Clubhouse, there are two that stand out and which I hope I
will never forget.

The first was simply this: if you feel God telling you to
do something, don't give up on it just because things are
getting difficult or doubtful. It is often the really important
things that prove hardest to persevere with to their successful conclusion. Might it be that this is because these are the
things that meet with the greatest opposition?

The other lesson that those 'young champions' taught us
both was that it is okay to be yourself. Don't change who you
are to try to be like me. I want to know who you are so I can
decide if I want to trust you with my friendship.

7.

Back to Africa

Meanwhile back at the day job, the everyday life of Jon and Tessa continued to move on. University life seemed at last to be starting to move in the right direction, as I finally began to develop a better understanding of things more scientific.

At around this time, Tessa took her Law Society Finals and the day came for the results to be published in *The Times*. Would those crucial two words appear in the columns of tiny print displaying the successful candidates for that year?

One advantage of living in central London was that it was always possible to pick up tomorrow's edition of the main papers from the forecourt of Victoria Station, if you went late enough, before they were shipped all over the country for sale on high streets from Land's End to John O'Groats, the following morning.

We waited until gone midnight before we buzzed over to Victoria on our trusty Kawasaki. I had secreted a champagne glass in each chest pocket of my motorcycle jacket and a bottle of bubbly in the back box, just in case. With trepidation we bought our copy of *The Times* and ripped it open right there under the station lights. We scanned the columns of tiny print and then Tessa shrieked and pointed to the page.

There they were. The two words that meant so much: '*Therese Cox*'. 'Fantastic!'

Somehow with all the other craziness going on in life with a wedding, two house moves, a busy extra youth ministry and getting used to being married to a guy like me, Tessa had also passed every section of the notorious Law Society Finals. We went for a celebratory spin around London. At one point we drove down Park Lane and over the Thames to visit our old house at Lambeth, France, before coming back over the river via Westminster Bridge. As we approached Big Ben and the Houses of Parliament I was suddenly aware that Tessa had stood up on the footrests behind me, and was saluting and singing the National Anthem at the top of her voice!

A Return Trip

As the second year of university wore on, I was encouraged to think about a suitable subject for a final year thesis. During our last visit to Canada, I had been in touch with the Ghanaian Pastor of the Churchill Baptist Church near Toronto. David, the Pastor, was very involved in a project to set up an orphanage and community farm in Northern Ghana and he had invited me to go out there for a summer to help with setting it all up.

My background as a health teacher and development worker in Sudan, coupled with my growing knowledge in Environmental Sciences, formed great preparation for the initial research into the needs of the local community and, more specifically, for assessing which crops would grow best on which parts of their thousand-acre farm.

The idea of the project was to provide a home for children orphaned by violence, sickness or poverty, and to use model agricultural methods on the farmland to feed all the children and the orphanage staff. In addition to providing them with a home and food, the children would also learn good agricultural practice which they would take with them to their villages, when they were old enough to return home. This was a great idea and both Tessa and I were keen to help where we could.

Stepping Out in Faith

However, there was the small matter of costs. How were two students living in London going to pay for return flights to Ghana? We decided to pray about whether or not we should go, and if so, for some help towards funding the trip.

What an encouragement it was when I discovered I was to be accepted for a Lightfoot Travel Scholarship, followed by a grant which came in from The Nuffield Foundation towards the costs of travel and assisting on the project. My expenses had been wonderfully met. What about Tessa's?

I discussed this with a friend who suggested approaching the church to ask if they would consider a short-term missions grant for Tessa. The first step was to get in touch with Dr June Morgan, a retired missionary and chair of the committee that decided on the allocation of support. As we were to appreciate on many future occasions, she was an immensely supportive friend and very aware of the pressures involved when setting out to follow the path that God sets in front of us, which is often, as American poet Robert Frost put it so well, 'the path less travelled'.

June encouraged us to apply for short-term mission support, asking us to fill out the relevant application and enclose a suitable photograph of Tessa.

Having completed the form I offered to post it, but could not resist enclosing three photos of Tessa including one of her relaxing in bed suitably equipped with the weekend papers and a platter of croissants; and one taken by Jim, my adopted Canadian dad when he took us out to try some of his not inconsiderable collection of firearms. It shows Tessa dressed in combat greens and armed with a Kalashnikov rifle and a large Bowie knife between her teeth!

Clearly Tessa needed to know which photos I had enclosed with her application but I did not tell her until after I had posted them. There followed an exchange of views which I tried to take as seriously as Tessa felt I should. But the mental picture of the Chair of the World Mission Committee opening her application to find two photos of her, one armed to the teeth in combat fatigues, the other lounging in bed with the Sunday papers, somehow distracted me from the gravity of the situation.

Fortunately the committee took my humour in the right way and, recognising the value of the project, decided to support our trip, funding nearly all of Tessa's return air fare. There was also a real lesson here for us both, which we would lean on time and time again in years to come: to learn to trust God when stepping out to do his work.

Machetes and Monsoons

So at the end of the summer term, we packed our bags and once more found ourselves belting up and watching the aeroplane safety briefing, this time en route to Accra. On arrival we were met by one of the Ghanaian team who looked after us during our time in the capital. It took just a few days to obtain the necessary travel permits, and soon we were loading our luggage and the equipment we would need for the next 8 weeks into the Hilux pick-up and taking the road inland to Kumasi and on, up to the Northern Region.

It was great to be back in Africa, and yet whilst so much felt familiar after our time in Sudan, Ghana was definitely a different country.

Our drive took us from the capital, north to Kumasi and the tropical rain forest belt. After a brief visit to the University, we headed north again into a drier and more arid region as we approached the regional capital, Tamale. We were to be staying in the nearby village of Walewale with Sayibu, the Ghanaian agriculturalist who was heading up the project, his lovely wife Somata, and their new baby, Wunpeni. We had already met Sayibu and Somata during our time in Ontario and they managed to make us feel very welcome, even though they had only just finished building their new house, the day before we arrived!

My main task was to clear and plant some test plots on different parts of the 1,000-acre site to see which crops would grow best where. What a fantastic opportunity for a practical outworking of my Environmental Science degree. The first job was to clear land for the test plots, which involved long days of hard physical labour under a scorching West African sun, working alongside a small team of workers, each of us equipped with local machetes. We would meet in the early morning, while it was still dark and share a bowl of highly spiced local Sorghum porridge, before setting out for the fields.

Meanwhile, Tessa was to use her time to interview the women of the local villages to identify their priorities for community development in the area. As the weeks progressed both aspects of our work were coming together well and we were made to feel a part of the local community. I even enjoyed the chance to play with a local High Life band, led by Sammi, the bank manager in the local town of Tamale.

Sleeping was not always easy, usually due to the combination of bugs, bites and the heat, especially in our tin-roofed house. One night we were kept awake for hours, but for a very different reason. It was pleasantly cool and the air was unusually clear of mosquitoes and other bugs, but the noise was deafening. We could hardly hear each other speak, even though we were lying right next to each other. The constant din came from the ceiling, right above our heads. It was raining. Hard!

This was the most torrential tropical storm I had ever seen, or heard, and it lasted for hours. Eventually the noise abated to a less oppressive level, sounding more like rain drops on a corrugated tin roof than a battery of industrial jack hammers pounding the house. Finally, we were able to get some sleep, and even to enjoy the cool of the fresh night air, following the storm.

More Than Rubies

When we awoke to a fresh new morning, it was amazing to see how the area had been transformed so quickly. There were large standing puddles everywhere but any vegetation that had survived the drought looked instantly fresh and green. We breakfasted and prepared to leave for the village of Janga, and another round of interviews for Tessa whilst I was heading out to take the next series of measurements of our test crops.

The journey along the only road to the village was not straightforward. A market lorry had slid off the side of the raised road and would not move again until a road grader could be brought out from Tamale so we had to head back to our home in nearby Walewale until the next day.

When we eventually made it out to the village to continue our work, I left Tessa to conduct more interviews with the local women and headed out to see how our test crops had survived the storm, hoping to see them revitalised by the recent rain. As we emerged from the undergrowth at the site of the first plot, our whole team stopped dead in its tracks. The neatly planted rows of cereals and ground nuts, which had been just starting to appear through the dry sub-Saharan soil, had been replaced by a small lake! Almost the whole plot had been wiped out by a flash flood.

We just stood there for some minutes surveying the scene. None of us could find the right words to say. All our work over the last five or six weeks lay under that beautiful still reflection of clear Ghanaian blue sky and vibrant green vegetation. There was no point in taking out our measuring gear, there was nothing to survey. Eventually we decided to go on to the next plot to see if that had fared any better.

As we walked the well-trodden path, I suddenly realised the implications for my university course. We had raised study grants and travel scholarships to come all this way to help the Janga Project and gather data for my final year thesis, and now it seemed this was all going to be a total washout – literally!

Approaching the next area I was encouraged to see that there was no lake. That was the good news! But the bad news became clearer as we got closer to the plot. This time the crops had simply been washed right away. There was hardly any evidence of any agricultural activity here at all. Again there was nothing to measure. No data to collect.

This story was repeated at each of our test plots and we returned down-hearted to the village where we found Tessa talking with a group of women at one of the local wells. Back at Sayibu's house we shared our disastrous news with him and asked how he'd like us to use our remaining time in Walewale. He wanted Tessa to continue her interviews and for me to begin a similar survey with the men in the community. But what was I to do about the research data for the final year thesis?

In the end, when we returned back to the UK it was the data from Tessa's interviews with the women of the villages that formed the basis of my final year dissertation. Yes, I had to face the fact that the vast majority of data for the major piece of written work in my final year at university had been gathered by my wife!

I, for one, would not argue with the writer of the Book of Proverbs in the Old Testament:

A wife of noble character who can find?
She is worth far more than rubies.
Her husband has full confidence in her

and lacks nothing of value.
She brings him good, not harm,
all the days of her life.
(Proverbs 31:10–12)

Proverbs concludes:

Honour her for all that her hands have done,
and let her works bring her praise . . .
(Proverbs 31:31)

Her works certainly helped convince the examiners at the end of my final year. Was it worth more than rubies? It certainly felt that way to me at what could otherwise have been a major personal crisis.

A Step of Faith

I have often been intrigued by the way we judge the age of people we do not know very well in our fast-paced Western society, especially when compared with cultures where comprehensive records are not kept and many cannot tell exactly how old they are. Their age is often determined by the status of the job they do.

The contrast with the UK came into sharp focus for me one evening towards the end of my final year at King's College. I was out with a few friends celebrating the end of exams. We must have been having a noticeably good time because some other people in the pub came over to ask us why we were in such high spirits. I explained that I had just had my last exam, and they congratulated me . . . on the completion of my A levels!

Well actually no, it wasn't my A levels. In fact, nearly four years previously, having already completed more than four years of training and work as casualty nurse, I had set up and then run an emergency field hospital in a war zone in East Africa, and at that time it had been assumed I must be at least 30 years of age, when I had in fact only been about 23. Since then I'd studied and had just completed a full three-year degree course, and was now 28. Their comment effectively showed that they thought I was about 18!

I don't claim to have the gift of eternal youth nor do I believe our behaviour was any more or less mature than others in the pub that night. This was just a great illustration of the assumptions people make about age and maturity which are so often linked to the roles we are fulfilling, which in this case was evidently not a very accurate gauge.

Decision Time

When the results were published I was surprised, and very relieved, to find that the hopeless arts student had managed to turn the situation around and get a good science degree. So here we were, aged 28, married and faced with a clear and formidable decision: grasp the nettle and throw ourselves at the challenge to somehow 'encourage people to live the adventure of faith', or do the sensible thing: build on a successful degree and get a proper, paid job, start a pension plan and get insured!

All normal impulses pulled us strongly towards the latter – we were newly married and by now Tessa was earning the humble wage of a trainee solicitor, known in the legal profession at the time as an Articled Clerk. And I had by some amazing miracle managed to pull off a respectable degree which could easily be a springboard into any number of different and potentially fulfilling career paths.

We also had a number of interesting conversations with Tessa's father at this time. Anyone who knew Bob would agree he was a man of solid principles, a healthy work ethic and a great encourager. His subsequent knighthood (Sir Robert Peliza) for services to Gibraltar and the Commonwealth, and the evident high esteem in which he was clearly regarded by his family and those who worked with him, are all testament to his admirable human qualities. He was, however, far from convinced about our apparent willingness to turn our back on building a career in order to trust God and follow his call on our lives.

We had many good-natured but challenging conversations around this theme, borne out of his concern for his daughter and her overly optimistic new husband. In some ways such conversations added to the pressures of this difficult step of faith, but in other ways, we saw this as a God-given natural opportunity to share what was at the heart of this 'calling'.

The underlying conviction that ultimately determined our decision was simple. We just could not ignore the memory of those remarkable events that led us to pray about how to use the encouraging experiences we'd had during those amazing months in Sudan. Then there were the strikingly clear answers to prayer, along with the unmistakable moments of divine guidance, we had been privileged to witness since:

- the unexpected comment from an old school friend, already disillusioned with life at the age of 23, that 'there has got to be more to life than this';
- the prayers which followed, accepting that if we were going to try to do something to encourage people to embrace the adventures of life and faith, we'd need contact with people engaged in this type of outreach;
- the out-of-the-blue appearance of Mike and Chris from Birch Bay Ranch the very next day, resulting in the invitation to spend such a formative summer with them in Alberta. The amazing opportunity to see first-hand how they are able to encourage such a wide range of young people in the long term, over their teenage years and into young adulthood.

It had certainly felt right at that time to continue with my degree course and Tessa with her Law Society Finals, whilst gaining valuable experience in youth work and starting to learn the basics of climbing and kayaking. And now here we were at the end of all that, and yet very much at the start of a project that could take years – a project to create the means to deliver adventure activities safely and legally in a UK setting, modelled on the best of what we had seen in Canada.

This was our vision and this was our passion – to offer exciting, fun activities for young people from a wide range of backgrounds that would inspire them to want to come back, year on year, and grow in an awareness that they are much loved and highly valued, and to help them realise that every single one of them has a positive contribution to make.

But how? A Bible verse which both challenged and encouraged me at the time was Ephesians 2:10. It describes how we have each been made unique, with our own mix of skills, talents and weaknesses, and how there is a lifetime of challenging roles for us to play, for which we are wonderfully suited.

If that is true of the young people and children we would be working with, it was, of course, true for us too. Tessa and I now also had the opportunity to pursue the path that he so clearly seemed to have set before us. We were at the point of decision.

Should I follow the advice I was now receiving from many quarters to use my degree to get a good job, forgetting about those apparent answered prayers and the challenge to live the adventure of faith? Or should we step up to the mark and go wherever the path might lead, trusting that we had indeed received God's guidance and that our sense of his calling was real and not just the product of our own imaginings?

8.

Legal Aid

A decision had to be made and in the end, and not without the odd earnest prayer, we decided to embrace the challenge and see where it might lead. After all, if part of the vision was about encouraging young people to 'live the adventure of faith', then surely we would need to be prepared to step out in faith ourselves, and go where we clearly felt him leading. After all, a 'do as I say, not as I do' leader is seldom inspiring! As someone remarked at the time, 'If you don't take that path less travelled, you will never know where it would have taken you, but you'll probably always wonder.'

The first step, it seemed to us, was to try to set up a registered charity, which would at least lend some credibility to this embryonic initiative, and would also provide a framework for our operations. Therefore, I wrote to the Charity Commission to let them know that I wanted to establish a new youth-work charity and asked them to send details of how I should go about this.

While I was preparing to throw my energies into this new and precarious venture, Tessa continued her legal training. But in this area too, things felt far from settled. She had been delighted to secure a place for her articles with a local firm in the West End of London, less than 10 minutes' walk from our flat, but the longer she worked there the less happy she became. She began to realise that some aspects of the work were far from exemplary, and some of the processes and procedures appeared to be decidedly unethical!

It was at just this time that Tessa felt she could not continue at this practice. She decided to seek advice from a solicitor she had found in a register of Christian Solicitors, who had a practice not too far away from us, also in the West End.

I will always remember the morning Tessa left the flat for the meeting in Red Lion Square. She had been very concerned how this process would unfold as it is not normally considered good practice to leave your articles part way through, and transfer to another firm. It was also on that very day that the large envelope from the Charity Commission fell onto the front door mat, with all the information I needed to set up a Registered Charity.

'Oh help!' I thought. 'Where do I start?'

As I began to leaf through the thick wodge of papers describing the process and requirements for setting up a new charity, the magnitude of the task descended on that ground floor flat like a heavy cloud. Proof was required that the charitable objects of the proposed organisation were indeed charitable in law and I had to wade through information about the different kinds of charities to decide where ours might fit. Then I was going to have to find suitable trustees who would be prepared to take this non-starter of an idea seriously enough to meet regularly, chart progress and create annual reports. We'd also need help to set up and keep approved accounts, and submit them in the required format at the end of the year. Then there was the formidable process itself. I honestly did not know where to start, or how best to go about it.

It was clear that this was going to take a huge amount of work before we could actually do anything constructive in terms of our actual mission – not least because these pages and pages of instructions were clearly all written before the Plain English Campaign had made any inroads into the publishing department of the Charity Commission!

As I sat in the shaded lounge of our flat on a dark autumn morning, I felt the first wave of reality hit home. Could this really be the right path? Surely there were others doing similar work here in the UK already. Why should we need to get involved? Was this the right time to be moving into such uncharted waters, when Tessa was also caught up in such an uncertain and disconcerting situation at her work?

The day wore on and I did my best to stick at reading through all the papers, making notes on the main tasks that lay ahead if we were really going to try to set up a charitable organisation from scratch. Eventually, as late afternoon drifted into evening Tessa returned and I was eager to hear how she had got on with her interview.

I was amazed at the change in her mood from the doubt and worry of the morning. She seemed strangely, unexpectedly encouraged. Yes, she had met with the solicitor, whose name was Tim, and he had listened and appeared to understand her situation. He had recognised that some of what Tessa was describing was clearly not best practice, and some of it sounded downright unprofessional.

He had also asked Tessa about her general background and towards the end of the meeting had enquired what her husband did for a living. When Tessa had mentioned our hopelessly embryonic plans to try to establish a youth adventure and education charity with a Christian ethos, he'd appeared to take a real interest. As the conversation unfolded, it became apparent that he just happened to be a regular member of Holy Trinity Brompton, the church which had developed the Alpha Course, and had a particular interest in youth work. He had also just set up a registered charity for another organisation. He wondered if Tessa might be interested in transferring her articles to his company, and if so, would we like his help in the whole process of establishing a charity.

Oh . . . and, he also *happened* to have spent much of his early life in Gibraltar, where Tessa had grown up, and had even attended the same convent primary school as Tessa, though admittedly a few years beforehand!

What were the chances? Another mere coincidence or further amazingly clear encouragement to us just when we needed it, that this was indeed the right path . . . 'Go in peace. The journey on which you travel is under the eye of the Lord.'

Needless to say, our whole doubtful outlook on this apparently foolhardy venture was transformed. Here we were, three years on, feeling it was right to try to build on those initial nudges which had originally guided us onto this path, but with no idea how practically to take it forward.

After such a time lapse it had felt like the trail had gone cold. There was no momentum at all and the massive administrative climb ahead, of which establishing a registered charity was just the first step, was daunting in the extreme. That morning there had been no discernible clear way forward – and no real offers of help with any of it. This completely unexpected meeting was both a major step forward and, just as important, a real endorsement for us, just when we were beginning to doubt our sanity, because it rekindled the sense that this was not just our own crazy, dreamed-up idea.

Once again we were witnessing an amazing answer to a prayer we had not even thought to pray and with it came a renewed sense of purpose and faith in all we had felt called to, so many years before. Here too was evidence of a God whose compassion reached into a lonely and doubtful situation, at a time when he knew how much we needed reassurance.

And in practical terms, this link with Tim Lawson-Crut-tenden, the solicitor who was shortly to become Tessa's principal, would prove pivotal in getting this project off to a credible start. He was a guy who knew what he was doing, and he was coming alongside a guy who clearly had no idea!

As someone once said, when you are considering whether or not it is right to follow a 'God-call' and you feel inadequate for the task: 'God doesn't need our ability. He needs our availability!'

Welsh Wisdom

It was clear that the whole process of establishing a registered charity could take months or even years, even with this wonderful boost of Tim's expert guidance. This was rammed home to us one evening when we received a call from a couple who had been trying to gain charitable status for a similar project in Derbyshire for nearly two years. They were still battling the system with no clear idea of how much longer it might take.

Tessa, in the meantime, made arrangements to transfer to Tim's practice and for him to become her principal for the remainder of her articles. While all this was happening, I busied myself by preparing some of the initial information that would be required for our charity application process. In addition, we felt it would be a very good use of time to find out what else was going on in the field of adventure provision with a Christian ethos in the UK.

It was just as Tessa was starting out in her new job as articled clerk to Tim's practice that I managed to borrow a car and head off into Wales via the Midlands for a few days to visit a number of Christian centres. I was amazed, when I arrived at the Pioneer Centre near Kidderminster, to find a Canadian flag waving proudly at the entrance. Although this was a UK organisation, they too had links with similar work in Canada and were looking to adopt a specific approach to youth ministry, working mainly with groups of young people.

My next stop took me right to the north-west corner of Wales, to the Christian Mountain Centre in Tremadog. I camped the night before the meeting with my good friend Graham Harris, who had been teaching me the basics of kayaking and climbing in London. He had been staying up in the area to do some climbing of his own. He joined me for the meeting where we were met by Norman Beech, the centre director, who gave lots of helpful advice about staffing a residential centre and the pros and cons of staff living on site. He also advised me to visit a man called Lorimer Gray, who had transformed the work of the Abernethy Trust in Scotland, since he had joined 15 years earlier, moving into the minister's manse in Nethybridge and developing it as an outdoor centre.

North to Scotland and More 'Industrial Espionage'

As soon as I got back from my Welsh fact-finding mission, I wrote to Lorimer and asked if I might visit. It was not long before another research trip was soon on the agenda. In addition to the meeting with Lorimer, I managed to arrange to call in at the Badenoch Centre in Kincraig en route to meet the centre manager, the Reverend John Lyall.

What a humble and gracious man I found him to be. He shared the value of such work and encouraged me to stay on the path we had set out on. John Lyall emphasised that we should not underestimate the value of visits to places of such beauty in the lives of the children and young people, and the lasting benefit of the personal challenge of the adventure activities they enjoy. Often when he spoke to young adults who had come back to his centre, sometimes bringing their own youth groups or families, they shared with him how important and life changing their visits to his centre had been when they were younger.

When he saw I was driving around this beautiful part of the Cairngorm National Park on my own he decided I would need some encouragement and inspiration to match the impressive mountain beauty. He gave me a present of two albums by Ian White, a Scottish singer-songwriter, who had set a selection of psalms to music.

It was with a lighter spirit and a renewed sense of purpose that I left that small centre, managed by such a big-hearted man. Ian White's setting of Psalm 95 caught that sense of refreshment perfectly as I played it in the car on my way to meet Lorimer Gray.

Abernethy Trust was a market-leading provider of residential outdoor education in Scotland. Under Lorimer's leadership they had even expanded to take on another two centres, at Ardeonaig, beside Loch Tay, and on the Isle of Arran.

When I arrived at Abernethy, it was immediately evident that this was a place with a clear focus and positive aims. The staff members were all in uniform, friendly and well presented. I made my way to reception and was shown to Lorimer's office. His beaming, welcoming smile dissolved my sense of total inadequacy, even when I had to explain our calling and our plans, and to answer questions about the people who were backing us: there weren't any! And our experience? We had none!

As Lorimer showed me round the beautiful 25-acre estate, past the canoe store, climbing walls and fleet of minibuses, I was both impressed and intimidated by the scale of work set before us – how could we ever seek to emulate anything like this?

Lorimer, however, has a well-deserved reputation as a great encourager, and is totally committed to this kind of outreach to young people. Looking back on that day, I certainly benefitted from his warm and genuine interest in our potential.

Some might have thought him a little optimistic as he filled me with advice about the best type of crockery to buy when we came to setting up our restaurant and the benefits of dehumidifiers over plain warmth in our drying rooms. However, of more immediate value was his advice about linking in with a superb organisation called CCI/UK, an association of Christian outdoor centres and conference centres which was to prove an invaluable source of networking and wisdom in the years to follow. He also suggested that whilst I was north of the border I should try to fit in a visit to their centre at Ardeonaig, and the director there, Phil Simpson.

I left Abernethy with a vision of what might be, many years hence, the reassurance that there were other people in the UK pioneering similar work with young people in the outdoors and a genuine offer of help as our journey progressed.

I had been staying with a great friend and colleague of my mother's in Rannoch and was due to head home from there the next day. Lorimer kindly arranged for me to visit Phil Simpson at Ardeonaig on the shores of Loch Tay, a major loch in the next river system down from Loch Rannoch and the River Tummel to its north.

Ardeonaig was clearly run in the same mould as Abernethy. A renovated hunting lodge, set in beautiful grounds and with a fantastic view from the main lounge down the loch towards Kenmore, where the River Tay leaves the loch and loops east and south to the sea at Perth 100 miles away.

Phil was equally generous with his time, giving me a tour of his centre, which he must have done for hundreds of visitors before and hundreds since. He still managed to show genuine interest in our elementary plans even though, I have since discovered, he had been visited, only days before, by at least two others exploring similar schemes. Phil echoed Lorimer's advice to link in with CCI/UK but decided on providing a much bigger perspective and some cautionary advice for Tessa and me at this early stage in our journey.

In essence, Phil shared that this kind of work often looks deceptively fun. Every brochure from any centre displays high-action colour images of excited children and happy young people enjoying adventurous activities in beautiful surroundings – in good weather! But the truth is that, as in any service industry, there is a lot of routine and behind-the-scenes preparation before the fun can begin. It is also not a lucrative way to earn a living.

'In short, Jonathan,' he advised, retaining his hallmark smile, 'if God is not telling you to do it, don't do it!'

Good advice, no doubt, for any walk of life. There was one big problem here for me, though. All the evidence so far had pointed to one clear conclusion: God *was* telling us to do it!

9.

Charity Begins at Home

Meanwhile, back at home, Tessa had settled in to her new firm and, while enjoying the mix of general practice, she also made time to start on our application for charity status. When I came back from my Scottish visit, we filled in and submitted all the relevant paperwork the Charity Commission had requested and quickly got into a pattern of dealing with any questions or concerns they raised.

Where we needed more advice, Tim, Tessa's principal, would guide her on the best way to proceed. I would write up what was required, gather any necessary evidence and courier it straight round to the Charity Commission Offices in Haymarket, often within a couple of hours.

I don't think our papers ever really got the chance to become hidden under the piles of other applications on the relevant desks and it soon became apparent that we were making real headway. Two key details needed to be decided upon, however, before the process could progress any further.

First, we were applying to establish a Charitable Trust and therefore, by definition, would need trustees. A minimum of three was required. Unsure of who to ask, we approached our student group leader, Alan Jenkins, marketing manager for the Chartered Institute of Management Accountants, and Madeleine Bartley, my godmother, who was very involved in her local church and a number of Christian initiatives in Central London. Tessa agreed to be the third trustee, and as I was now committing myself to work full time to get things going, I would assume the title of 'Director'.

The second important detail was the name we were to give the organisation. This was quite a key decision as the name would do a lot to determine how people would view our work, both now at its inception, and into the future. Our aim was not to work solely with church groups or Christian young people, so we did not want an overly Christian name that might discourage local-authority youth workers or Social Services from working with us. We were also very aware that we were starting absolutely from scratch, and it might be very difficult to attract support, so a name that did not make us sound too novitiate might be wise, and in any case we'd have this name for many years to come. I often found myself praying about this and we asked many people for their ideas.

The process was not made any easier by the fact that we did not have a geographical identity, nor did we yet know which way our work might develop, so could not link the name, for example, to water sports, mountain expeditions or urban extreme sports.

In the end, it was a mental picture of an open clearing in a dark tangled wood that seemed to best capture our ethos of bringing light and clarity into the chaotic lives of young people. An important feature of the image in my mind was a shaft of sunlight shining down into the clearing and illuminating it and all who came into it, bringing clarity and light and dispelling the confusion of the darker world around. The name we settled on was 'The Fair Glade Trust'.

Out of the Comfort Zone

It was just before the Christmas break when we received a surprise phone call from our case officer at the Charity Commission to informally advise us that our application had been provisionally approved, but that we could not start to operate as a Registered Charity until we had received written confirmation, together with our Charity Number. This, we were told, could take up to three months.

It was with a real sense of being on the verge of an epic life adventure that we headed home to spend time with our families for Christmas. As we grew accustomed to the idea that we might have just succeeded in starting our own charitable organisation, another big question began to loom large: what now?

Many of the charitable outdoor centres that I have got to know since, were the inspiration of a businessman or landowner wanting to use their property for a lasting beneficial purpose. This was not the case for us. We would have to somehow make things happen without a wealthy supporter and without land for our centre.

It was clear that we would need some money to kick-start our work, so we started to explore how we might raise funds, often discussing it with friends who were beginning to take an increasing interest in what we were doing. A fund-raising club seemed like a good first move so we hit upon the idea of 'CLUB 111'. We would aim for 111 members, each of whom would agree to raise £111 per year towards the emerging

Mobile Health Clinic in Sudan. Showing Peter, our health care assistant and interpreter, how to spot signs of anaemia

Unexpected solutions . . . our water carrier came in the form of a fire engine . . . *from Legoland?*

Adventure Camp. All the kit was packed in the Birch Bay Ranch vans and we headed for the Rockies.

The van I called about turned out to be the old Great Britain Canoe Team minibus!

Windsurfing instruction with SU Salcombe

Total Adventure takes off and the climbing wall is a hit!

A+ is about getting young people out there to grow in self-confidence and live 'Life to the Max'.

A recent addition to the programme – Total Adventure Ski, in the Swiss Alps around Wengen, for our gap year team and campers.

Mountain skills training at the top of Bristly Ridge, North Wales.

The roles were clear for Witney2Westminster 2013 . . .
Lucy was the skipper – Dad, the engine room.

By HMS Belfast and Tower Bridge. What an experience, canoeing
from rural Oxfordshire into the heart of London.
Why not join us next time?

Occasionally we manage to get the whole family to an A+ event, including my mum.

Unusual headgear for central London.

It is wonderful to have a growing team of supporters, pictured here at Windmill Farm.

Our vans are a lot smarter now.

Jon and Tessa (above)
and A+ canoe coaches (below).

Will you help us as we work to challenge even more young people to 'live the adventure of faith'?

Loch view. There's peace as well as excitement to be found in 'the great outdoors'.

Jonny joined the A+ Gap Year team, and now he's paddling
Hell Hole . . . *backwards? Yay!*
The 'Out There – *In Him*' part of the gap year course takes us out
there . . . to reflect on the hand of our Creator, in his creation.

work of the Fair Glade Trust, once we finally received formal approval and a charity registration number.

We were definitely picking up momentum now and there was an unmistakeable buzz of excitement, but there was also something less positive in the air. We noticed quite a few friends were apparently puzzled and some quite concerned about what I was up to. How much was I being paid all this time? What about our plans as a young married couple? And what if we wanted to start a family? Who would be the bread-winner if Tessa had to stop work?

Often such questions were brought up in conversation with Tessa when I was not around. Was she happy that her husband was not earning any money? There was real poten-tial here to magnify the worries and dampen the energy and enthusiasm we'd need if we were to make it through this vulnerable exploratory phase.

Although we were both completely together in our convic-tion that this was the right thing, the repeated questioning did not help dispel the constant awareness that this was indeed an unusual approach to early married life. Although the motivation behind the concern was doubtless not intended to discourage us, there was a sense of growing pressure that this was perhaps not the wisest course for a young couple.

Tessa and I discussed this at length at the time: were these friends feeling uncomfortable, and possibly even a little challenged, because we were stepping out of *their* comfort zone, and into an adventure? Whatever the reason behind it, we were left in no doubt we had taken the 'path less travelled' and in many ways, at least humanly speaking, we were on our own in that.

We've Done It!

One morning in February 1990, an envelope dropped through the letter box of our ground floor flat from the Charity Commission. The Fair Glade Trust (FGT) had been registered as charitable organisation 802659 in the UK, to offer adventure and education in the interests of Education, Social Welfare, and to 'further the Christian Religion' – another reminder to us that this was all still before the plain English campaign! That was it. We were off.

Now what on earth were we going to do? Two priorities immediately sprang to mind. First we needed to get the word out about Fair Glade Trust and CLUB 111, and second we had to try to gain some support for me so I could continue to commit my efforts to this project full time. As so many had rightly pointed out, I was not being paid and I had now been engaged full time for nearly six months trying to get this project off the ground.

While all this was going on, our involvement in the Clubhouse continued, both as volunteer youth workers and members of the Sunday congregation. In addition, I remained a regular member of the brass section of the All Souls Orchestra. It therefore seemed appropriate to approach Dr June Morgan of All Souls' World Mission Committee to ask if they might once again consider supporting us in this new calling. As I walked the 10 minutes from Grafton Mews to Dr June's flat just off Devonshire Street, there was a sense that this was to be a meeting of great significance.

We sat down in her lounge over a cup of tea and I remember desperately trying to formulate all that had happened into a coherent, manageable conversation. I began falteringly trying to capture, but not labour, the background to the project and the signs of God's guiding hand along the way: starting with Sudan, the conversation with the friend who was bored with life at 23, Birch Bay Ranch, the Clubhouse, learning about outdoor pursuits and finally Tessa's move to work with Tim, together with all the help he gave in putting together our charity application.

Now here we were at the point where we had a legal organ-isation which needed my concerted efforts to get it going. Might this be work which All Souls would consider supporting us in? This was a completely different field and setting from their previous support for us, in rural community development first in East, then in West Africa and I had absolutely no idea how they would view this manifest change of direction.

June listened carefully and when I had shared all that I had wanted to get across she simply thanked me for coming and said she would take it to the church's Mission Commit-tee. She'd be back in touch when they had had a chance to consider our application. In the meantime, perhaps I could write up the key points I had shared and where I saw the project progressing into the future.

As I left June's flat, I was very aware that the result of this friendly chat would have huge implications for my ability to stay committed to this work full time in the coming months, and possibly even for many years to come.

CLUB 111

The other financial aspect that needed attention was the need to raise funds to get the work started – though we were still trying to sort out what exactly that might mean. Our good friends, Andrew and Rachel Baughen, among others, agreed to help organise the launch of CLUB 111. All Souls were generous enough to give us the use of rooms in their sister church, St Paul's, and about sixty guests were invited to an evening of 'pizza, games and inspiration'. That night, over thirty signed up to join CLUB 111, agreeing to raise £111 in whatever way they thought most appropriate to them, or to start regular giving of £10 per month.

We already had a properly formulated Code of Conduct and guiding document, aptly titled the 'CLUB 111 Consternation', with 11 key paragraphs which included:

1: CLUB 111 has no legal standing whatsoever; it is purely an agreement amongst friends.

4: Members of CLUB 111 will undertake to raise £111 towards the work of Fair Glade Trust by any means they choose, provided that it is not illegal, neither uncouth nor unbecoming of the finest spirit of CLUB 111.

9: CLUB 111 welcomes associate members from other countries who may establish separate chapters in their own country.

10: It shall be the honour and duty of CLUB 111 member number 111 to read the 'Consternation of the Rules of CLUB 111', together with any other important preamble, at the start of each AGM, unless s/he doesn't want to.

11: The End

It was in this earnest spirit of Pythonesque humour that the first fund-raising efforts of Fair Glade Trust and ultimately

Adventure*Plus* were born and 34 founder members set about supporting this new and still very green venture. Earliest fund-raising efforts included a London Marathon run by Tessa's brother John, and a trek to Everest's base camp by CLUB 111 member 007, Graham Harris.

Issue 2 of the CLUB 111 Review, from the summer of 1990 is a reminder that fund-raising started to take a wide variety of creative turns:

'Strangeways' to raise funds

Those of you watching BBC news on Friday 11 May might recall a fleeting glimpse of a man locking himself in the tower of a parish church in Hertfordshire for charity . . . for four days!

Member number 011, Andrew Downes, took his mobile phone up the tower with him and called several local radio stations to gain support for his efforts, and to provide for all his needs. One emergency was solved by a listener to Radio Bedfordshire who heard Andrew's desperate appeal for a portable loo to be taken up the tower as a matter of urgency. The listener heard the radio appeal and drove straight home to pick up his Portapotty which he took straight to the church and negotiated up a very tight spiral staircase and ladder – to get the emergency equipment to the self-incarcerated prisoner . . . just in time!

Fund-raising creativity was clearly spreading far and wide with some very innovative schemes!

Other notable approaches included the youth group and leaders linked to Scripture Union's Salcombe Camp, who had been in touch with British Airways and arranged for CLUB

111 to clean a BAC 111 Aircraft; a journey from London to Land's End via local bus services (it took 5 days); an A to Z of the UK: a tour of place names beginning with every letter of the alphabet, in alphabetical order in a Morris Traveller; 'swimathons'; fund-raising concerts; hot-air ballooning; a CLUB 111 ball and a charity cricket match.

It was also about this time that I was invited back for a follow-up cuppa with Dr June Morgan, now CLUB 111 member number 041, to be told the thrilling news that the World Mission Committee at All Souls had decided they would indeed support our work and would be adopting us both as Mission Partners! A huge encouragement to us both as I continued to pursue this calling full time.

With such a wave of enthusiastic fund-raising support from CLUB 111, and then this endorsement and promise of support from our church, the sense of going it alone was soon eclipsed by the rapid acceleration of activity.

Location, Location, Location

Life, however, marched on regardless and Tessa was now approaching the end of her articles. This meant she would need to start applying for her first job as a newly qualified solicitor in the very near future, which would have a direct bearing on our progress with Fair Glade Trust. If she applied for a job in London we would then be tied to the city for a further two or three years, so ideally we wanted to move to the right location from which to launch our first activities. But where would that take us? What was the 'right location'?

Our clear plan from the start had been to find an area roughly 90 minutes from Central London, to be accessible for youth groups from the city, without the ordeal of the four-hour minibus ride on a Friday evening to get to the more conventional areas for adventure activities such as The Lakes, Snowdonia, the Brecon Beacons or the West Country.

We knew that for young people living in the city, just getting away from their urban environment and from peer pressure in school or on their estate, makes a huge difference. It's not always necessary to travel all the way to a National Park or a mountainous region, and introductory canoe sessions certainly do not require roaring rapids to make them exciting – far from it! Experience was to show that just being in a place that actually gets dark at night, or walking through a field with a large number of sheep in it, can often provide adventure enough for the most hardened urban clients!

So we started in earnest to look for a suitable location within 70 miles of the Telecom Tower, with access to water for introductory water sports, and reasonable transport links to Central London. Our research soon showed that the many lakes around the M25 perimeter would prove far too costly for our charitable plans to offer 'affordable, accessible adventure'. We visited a possible property in Essex and also had meetings with Brian Betts, the warden of Ashburnham Place, a Christian Conference Centre set in stunning grounds, with lakes, to the south of London, near Battle, but it was felt our youth adventures might clash with the quieter retreat focus of Ashburnham Place at the time.

Throughout this period we had asked our growing band of supporters, including our seventy or so CLUB 111 members, to be praying for specific direction for FGT. As the weeks ticked by this was becoming more urgent for us, because Tessa's date for qualification was now fast approaching.

We were grateful to a number of friends at the time who generously invited us to dinner, with a number of their other guests, and asked us to share our plans with them, to try to enlist more support for FGT and possibly nudge up the membership of CLUB 111. One evening, we were invited to the home of two friends, Rachel and Philip. They had one other guest that night, a Canadian, called Dawn, who was visiting them at their home in Kew, West London. Inevitably our fledgling plans for 'Adventure with a purpose' became a topic of conversation around the dinner table, not least our pressing need to decide where the next move would take us.

As that part of the conversation drew to a close, Philip, our host for the evening, challenged us:

'If you really want to mobilise support for this work, people are going to need a location and a direction to focus on. It will be increasingly difficult to get people motivated if you don't know where you are going, and they cannot visualise with you the right way forward. And anyway, if God is really behind this then he already knows where he wants you to go. So why don't we pray about it this evening, and ask God for his clear direction for his work at FGT?'

Of course we had already been praying for weeks about the right next move and where Tessa should apply for her first solicitor's job, but what Philip had said made good sense and a little more prayer is always a good plan. So we prayed together around that dining table specifically for his guidance on the right next move for FGT. Once we'd finished praying and the evening was drawing to a close, Dawn said that while we had been praying she had heard a word quite clearly and she felt she ought to share it. We had never met this lady before, and have not seen her since. She looked quite sheepish and admitted that actually it wasn't a proper word at all, and it meant nothing to her, and we'd probably think she was mad, so . . .

'Well tell us the word anyway,' I encouraged her.

'But it doesn't even mean anything. It's just that I heard it so clearly,' she said.

'We won't mind if it doesn't mean anything to us either,' I said. 'It's okay, just say it.'

'Okay then. The word I heard was "Windrush".'

Tessa and I looked at each other with completely blank expressions on our faces. 'Well, thanks for sharing that. I can't say it means anything to us either, but we'll bear it in mind,' I began to reply, when a slightly abrupt interruption was heard from Rachel, our hostess.

'What did you say?'

'Windrush,' Dawn said again.

'The Windrush Valley in Oxfordshire is about 90 minutes from central London, and we know the mayor of a town called Witney, which is built on the River Windrush!' Rachel said. 'Maybe you should go and meet him!'

The next day I made a completely 'out of the blue' call to Councillor Andrew Carter, the Mayor of Witney and Senior Partner at A.J. Carter and Co., a firm of accountants in Witney High Street, 500 metres from the River Windrush. I explained why I was calling and I must have somehow managed to convince him that I was not completely barking mad, because he invited me up to visit him the following week and suggested I set up a meeting whilst I was there with one of the planning officers at West Oxfordshire District Council.

So the next week I borrowed a car from Alan, one of our Trustees, and made my first journey out of London to visit the unknown town of Witney, built on the River Windrush. The drive took approximately 90 minutes!

10.

Windrush

The River Windrush rises deep in rural Gloucestershire, from a tiny spring near the village of Cutsdean. This idyllic, wavering little stream flows lazily south-east through classic Cotswold stone villages such as Guiting Power, Temple Guiting and Naunton, gradually growing in size and beauty alongside more substantial and abidingly picturesque villages which have sprung up along its banks over the centuries: Bourton on the Water, Windrush Village, and The Barringtons. Burford, whose main street is drawn down the side of the valley by the river and by its high-steepled St Mary's Church, stakes her claim as 'the gateway to the Cotswolds'. Seven miles downstream from Burford you arrive at the busy, charming market town of Witney.

I had approached Witney from the other side, leaving central London after the main flood of rush hour traffic had died down. I joined the Euston Road just 2 minutes from our flat at Warren Street and headed west, past The Royal Academy of Music, Madame Tussauds and Baker Street Station. I am still amazed by, and grateful for, this fast track out of London. From here, right in the heart of our capital city, the Marylebone Flyover whisks drivers up and over the mesh of traffic

lights and junctions of West London, and deposits them onto
a dual carriageway. Next stop Oxford!

Am I indulging in a digression here? Maybe, but for me
this is a recognition that the plans God had all along have
proved so much better, for so many reasons, than plans we
might have come up with ourselves. This 'expressway' into
central London was to become a much-travelled route when
we finally moved to Oxfordshire, travelling back into London
to develop more links with youth agencies, supporters and
churches in the city. I cannot imagine how many hours it has
saved over the years.

It was in a surprisingly relaxed frame of mind that I arrived
in Witney for the first time, earlier than expected, and piqued
with anticipation of the potential adventures that might lie in
store here in future years.

It soon became apparent that the Windrush was central
to the town. As I arrived in Witney, I drove over the River
Windrush and saw signs to the Windrush Industrial Estate
and the Windrush Press. Later in the day, as I was leaving
Witney, I also drove past the Windrush Pub! It was hard to
believe that I had lived all my 27 years within 90 minutes'
drive of this place and had never even heard the name before,
until that evening when Dawn had shared, quite unexpectedly, that she'd heard the word 'Windrush' from God!

Having parked the car, opposite the Windrush Leisure
Centre of course, I received directions to the High Street and
found the Offices of A.J. Carter and Co. As Andrew Carter
came out to meet me, I was not entirely sure how to explain
why I was here, without sounding hyper-spiritual, completely
naïve or totally deluded.

All I could do was share my story, which he was gracious enough to listen to. He then commented that Witney was probably the ideal location for our plans. Not only was it 90 minutes' easy drive from Central London, but just to the south of the town was a network of over twenty lakes, which were the result of excavations for the M40 and other major developments in the region. Knowing I had set up a meeting with the District Planning Department, also based in Witney, that afternoon, he kindly invited me to his home to meet the rest of his family that evening.

My meeting with West Oxfordshire District Council's Planning Department was next. How was I to frame our plans to establish a purpose-built adventure centre for young people in the area and further afield, knowing that we had no money with which to do it, without sounding hopelessly unhinged?

Once again I met with a generous and understanding response. There were indeed a number of lakes and our vision of small-scale development, with moderate activity-related accommodation in wooden cabins, would certainly be an approach that would fit with development plans for the area.

I left the offices with an invitation to get back in touch if, in fact, we decided to base our work in West Oxfordshire. As I journeyed back to our London flat to share news of the day with Tessa, I knew that I had glimpsed a sneak preview of the next stage in the trail which was opening up before us.

A 'Need-to-Know' Basis

As I made further visits to Witney and continued my exploration, we were amazed how many threads were falling into place. It quickly became clear to Tessa and me that this journey between London and Oxford was going to become a regular event in the weeks and months to come.

However, it was now less than three months until Tessa was due to finish her articles, which would complete her legal training, so the time was fast approaching for her to start applying for her first job as a solicitor. We were faced with a quandary: to apply right where we were in London, which definitely felt like the safe option, or move on, in faith that 'Windrush', which we had never even heard of until less than a month ago, was indeed a word of guidance from God; and move west to Oxfordshire.

To apply and get accepted in London would certainly have held things up as far as going proactive with our plans to start delivering 'adventure with a purpose' for young people. But to move out and away from all our friends and family, a church we were really involved in, and the young people we had got to know over the past three years, would be a real wrench, and all on the basis of one word, even a word given in a time of prayer?

Whilst there was no doubt in our minds that God had given us the word 'Windrush' in the nick of time, there was one final piece of the puzzle that needed to fall into place if we were to be able to act on this amazingly clear guidance from on high, and it would dictate the course of our lives for years to come.

We were talking with a friend about the increasingly urgent need to hear from God and his comment seemed particularly pertinent: 'God tends to let his people know his plans on a need-to-know basis.' That may be true, but our sense of urgency was growing and our need to know was certainly growing with it.

The Final Piece of the Jigsaw

We have always felt that as he has called us into the next phase of this journey, especially at the points when there has been a big step to make, God has been gracious in giving us big hints that have been too clear to ignore. Now, as we wrestled with the decision to move away or stay settled where we were, we felt a particular need for clarity on the right way forward. It was a similar need for reassurance that we'd felt at the point of my decision not to seek paid employment after graduating, or at the decision to start the process of applying for Charity status.

To move away from London, on nothing more than the word of a lady we'd never even met, felt very committing. It was a very tangible step down the road away from all that was familiar, and on into the adventure ahead. But as we further explored the Windrush Valley trying to assess if it was the right location to put down our first roots and start to build an adventure outreach for young people, so many things seemed to fall into place. Of course there had been that remarkably clear guidance through the quite unexpected word 'Windrush' in the first place, which was absolutely in line with our vision for a rural location 90 minutes from Central London.

It also had the added benefit of being approximately 90 minutes from the other great centre of population in the UK, Birmingham. It is humbling to have to admit that I had not thought of this before, but from this point of view –

west of London and south of Birmingham was the obvious choice!

Then we'd had the introduction and remarkably warm welcome from the Mayor of Witney, built on the River Windrush. In addition, there was the small matter of the presence of over twenty lakes in the immediate area, and a planning office who welcomed the idea of small-scale development of recreation and leisure use of these lakes!

All this seemed too clear to ignore and we had no hints that God was pointing towards a different path. So what were we to do now?

One factor remained unresolved, and without it we would not be able to move to this wonderful area that seemed to hold all the answers. The final clincher would be the provision of a job for Tessa, which if all these signs were to mean anything, would need to be in Witney, or pretty close, especially as Tessa was not a driver at that stage. If a door opened up for her into a law firm there, then we felt we had more than enough to go on, and we'd progress to the next level.

Tessa duly checked the Law Society Gazette to see if there were any vacancies for a newly qualified solicitor in the Witney area. There were none. So she decided to write to all the firms of solicitors in Witney, even though none were advertising a vacancy, to ask if they might consider taking on a newly qualified solicitor. A sheaf of letters was written and sent off.

We only needed one reply, but we got three inviting Tessa to come for an interview. Another day visit to Witney, this time with Tessa, resulted in her being offered a job with the established Witney firm, John Welch and Stammers. This was the final piece in the jigsaw. A door had opened. It was time to vote with our feet and put our faith into practice.

In short, it was time to move.

Woodland Therapy

We were now catapulted into a frenzy of activity to make the move happen. We wound up our involvement at the Clubhouse, gave notice on our rented flat and explored the possibility of a house we might be able to afford in Witney.

I won't recount here the details of our move. Instead, I want to describe one particular weekend just before we left London which seemed to offer a glimpse of some of the benefits of the adventures ahead. I had been asked to be a minibus driver for a weekend away to Hastings for one of the youth clubs. We took a group of about ten young people down on a Friday night and camped close to the beach. Activities on the weekend included going into Hastings, an evening at the fair and time on the pier amusements.

The weekend was for the most part a positive event but I had a strong sense that as we came out of the city, it would be really good to try to enjoy a few hours in the countryside, away from the bright busyness of the town. There was not really time to write this into the programme but on the way home the guys were happy to go with my suggestion to pull off the A21 into a quiet area of woodland, just to chill and maybe take a short walk.

Although on the face of it nothing particularly dramatic happened, there was an almost unmistakeable change in the mood of the group when we got out of the bus and found ourselves immersed in the quiet beauty of the woods on a sunny afternoon. We did not have long before we had to get back on board and head for London, but I had witnessed the advantages of a woodland or wilderness experience in the lives of urban young people. A number of them even sought me out during the following week to thank me for making the detour.

It is interesting that quite a lot has been written since about the benefits of such experiences, in the low pressure settings of beautiful woodlands, rivers or mountains to young people who would not normally have access to this kind of space, amidst the relentless pressures of modern life.

The term 'Nature Deficit Disorder', coined by American author Richard Louv in his book *Last Child in the Woods*, captures both the need for, and the many benefits of, such an experience. Tessa and I were eager to begin our work of offering youngsters, especially perhaps those from an urban background, adventures and encouragement in a rural environment, where they could receive a break from the pressures of everyday life, as well as a brief taste of the wonderful, healing properties of being out in the beauty of God's creation.

A Big Move

So a plan to prepare to move from London began to take shape. However, we could not immediately see how we would be able to afford a deposit to rent, much less buy, a house or flat in Oxfordshire on Tessa's newly qualified solicitor salary and the support I received for my work of developing the Fair Glade Trust.

Every week we would scour the Property News for something that might be affordable, but we also looked at the possibility of living on a caravan site, just to get a foothold in the area. Our absolute ceiling in our budget at the time was the grand total of £60k, with a 100% mortgage. When we saw a three-bedroom ex-council house for sale for £59,950, we wasted no time in getting up to see it and putting in an offer, and by the time Tessa's articles in London were complete, we found ourselves with a house to move into and a first real job for her.

The final journey from our flat in Grafton Mews out to Witney, in a van jam-packed with all our possessions, including an upright piano, will always be etched on my memory. If you ever drive from London to Oxford on the M40, after about forty minutes you will find yourself at a point in the road where the banking on both sides rises steeply as the road drops down, cutting through the ridge which marks the western edge of the Chilterns.

As our van emerged from 'the cut', we suddenly found ourselves looking out over the wide expanse of the Thames Valley stretched out below as far as the eye could see. I knew we were looking out across the land that would become the backdrop for our future adventures with Fair Glade Trust, our continued journey together as a couple and maybe even the start of a new family.

Our journey to Oxford had become a graphic illustration of what was to become the primary theme of our youth camps. It had become an adventure of faith, an adventure that we were being called to live before calling others to embrace it.

Here We Go . . .

We were now in our new home. We had made the move, from close friends and a supportive church out to the town of Witney. Apart from the Mayor, our good friends from All Souls and CLUB 111 members Jonathan and Penny Marks (who had moved to nearby Eynsham), we knew no one. For me the canvas was, if anything, too blank.

Tessa started to settle into her new professional life, learning skills and picking up more knowledge as a solicitor. Her nights as the Duty Solicitor on call for Witney Police Station were certainly an insight into this apparently happy market town. Once each month the calls were routed to our home phone and she would get up in the middle of the night and make her way to the police cells to represent another party animal brought low by alcohol. Her daily duties included a very varied caseload, a superb grounding for a newly qualified lawyer in general practice, and provided excellent experience for any legal issues that might come up as our organisation developed.

But how was I to be proactive with Fair Glade Trust? Which young people should we start to work with and where was I to take them? We had no venue, no stores, no equipment and no qualifications! We did however still have the encouragement, and the pressure too, of a great team of supporters: by now CLUB 111 had over fifty members.

Our First Residential Event

One charismatic character I'd got to know through a link with Christians in Sport was former Chicago Bears quarter-back,

Steve Connor. He had been working to set up a league of American Football teams in South London, and he wanted to bring the young people out of London for a weekend of sport and activity.

When he contacted me to see if the young people and the youth leaders of All Saints Brixton could come out to us in Oxfordshire, I got busy organising a place for them to stay and planning the programme.

As they were going to be coming out in the Easter Holidays, I contacted a local boarding school set in sixty-plus acres of beautiful parkland and sports fields. I was grateful to the headmaster at the time, Mr David Crawford, for considering and agreeing to my request that we bring up to forty young people to stay for a long weekend and use their dorms, dining rooms and sports facilities, all at a reasonable price.

As the days approached for our first residential event, all the plans for the programme, the travel and the catering were coming together really well. However, I realised I had not heard much at all from the school for some weeks. I decided it would be a good idea to write to confirm that we were planning to bring our group of forty from All Saints Brixton, and emphasised how much they were looking forward to it and what an important date it was in their annual programme of sport.

The day after I had delivered the letter to Cokethorpe School, I received a letter in the post from the head stating that at a recent staff meeting they had decided not to allow the group to come after all. The tone of this letter indicated that this was a fixed, terminal decision.

My heart sank. This was our first ever youth event; we had lined up volunteers and arranged transport. Parents had paid their contribution to the costs and the weekend had been publicised as a special, not-to-be-missed event around the youth football league in South London. Now here we were at a dead end!

A Welcome U-Turn

What now? I clearly had to contact the school to try to unpick the situation and retrieve our deposit, if nothing else, but this was a major blow, both to me and to the team at All Saints Brixton. The only thing we could do, in addition to contacting the school, was to pray about the situation: 'Lord, please let this totally unexpected U-turn decision, keep turning. We need a 360° turn around here. Please!'

The next day, a follow-up letter arrived, again with the familiar franking mark of Cokethorpe School. The headmaster had just received my letter, confirming the dates that our group was due to arrive, thanking him and pointing out that this was such an important event for these young people and their leaders. In light of this, he had generously decided to let the weekend go ahead as planned.

To this day, I'm grateful to the headmaster for allowing us to bring these young football teams out of London to his school. The young people who came were thrilled to have what turned out to be a positive and significant weekend of sport, fun and encouragement. Many of them were to come back to future FGT events for years to come and some are still in touch with us today.

The young people who emerged from the coach when it pulled up in front of Cokethorpe's impressive Queen Anne mansion were excited to have arrived at their long-awaited American Football training camp. They were not to know that as they stepped off the bus, they were also marking the beginning of a journey for us – the beginning of a journey that we had already been travelling for over three years.

11.

Sea, Sand and SU Salcombe

Another event which was to play a key part in enabling us to get things off the ground took me away from Oxfordshire, to the breathtaking location of the Salcombe Estuary in Devon.

SU (Scripture Union) Salcombe Camp was the name of an annual event that transformed a fairly ordinary, almost level, agricultural pasture into accommodation and an adventure HQ for up to 150 young people and leaders.

I had heard about this camp a couple of years earlier from my mother who had met the SU Salcombe leaders when she had spoken at their church. Having had no background at all in adventure holidays or Christian summer camps when I was growing up, I did not know what to expect when I made the journey down to the camping field for the first time.

I arrived for the work party weekend, 2 days before the camp was due to begin. I had been told what I needed to bring to stay comfortable for nearly two weeks in a scout tent with one other leader and six 'Senior campers'. My job on the team was 'Senior Camper Leader'. I had no idea what this might entail other than that the Senior Campers were in charge of 'the Lats', a euphemistic term for the camp toilets.

It was difficult to believe that the piles of poles, canvas and adventure kit would all be transformed into accommodation for 150 leaders and campers over the coming 2 days. At least there was a marquee and two smaller standing tents already in place, but there was clearly a massive job ahead of us all to create functional, even safe accommodation and washing facilities for so many.

Teens, Tents and Toilets

We all arrived in time for lunch for what turned out to be a slightly inauspicious start for me. As a rookie, it was difficult to know how to fit in as everyone else seemed to know each other. However I did notice one guy on the other side of the small marquee who was clearly also there for the first time so I wandered over to say hello. I discovered his name was Hudson Owen, from Frinton-on-Sea, and we quickly began talking about our respective roles at SU Salcombe for the coming 2 weeks.

Hud said that he was there to lead the windsurfing. He certainly fitted the bill, standing there, cool and relaxed, in his hoodie and Quiksilver boardies. I felt more than a little inadequate as I said, 'My name's Jon and I'm in charge of the lats!'

As it turned out the SU Salcombe leaders were all very welcoming and we all got to know each other as we laboured side by side putting up over twenty scout tents, constructing an ablutions block from a selection of corrugated plastic sheeting, canvas walls and a DIY plumbing kit. All planned to perfection and, thankfully, very effective.

It really was an impressive operation and I have rarely had the privilege of working alongside a more committed and focused team, under the wise, uncompromising yet unassuming leadership of Alan and Christine Sanders. The work party may not have been an easy way for volunteers to spend the first 2 days of their annual leave, but the result was a smooth, good-natured and well-planned system which kept the whole camp safe, clean and very well fed for the next 2 weeks.

The kitchen system was probably what impressed me most. The catering team managed to put out superb meals day after day for all 150 of us, without the benefits of mains water, gas or electricity. There were therefore no fridges, industrial mixers or even sinks with running water. In fact the entire water supply for the camp was piped in from a water junction two fields away and distributed to taps around the field. This single hose had to supply the water not only for the cooks but also for the washing up and for all the showers and wash basins.

I have since planned and led many adventure holidays in a variety of settings. They are always hard work but invariably rewarding and worthwhile, and in a strange way refreshing too. Many of these events have seemed at least as hard to organise, and yet they were nearly all within the setting of a school or residential centre, which enjoyed the comforts of industrial catering kitchens, hot showers and flushing toilets. I am still amazed as I look back at the sheer logistical achievement that was SU Salcombe. The vision and drive to deliver excellent adventure activities, which included rock climbing, snorkelling, sailing and sea kayaking, whilst providing clear ongoing Christian encouragement to teenagers and young adults year after year, was hugely impressive. The impact of these summer camps on so many young people through the rest of the year, and for the rest of their lives, was evident. Their work over decades gave us a brilliant example to follow.

'Lat'itude

The reality of that work party and training weekend was soon to hit home. I had known when I arrived that the Senior Camper leader was to be in charge of the 'lats'. This had not meant too much to me when I agreed to take on this task over the phone and read it in the pre-camp briefing.

Apparently there were no toilets on site so the sanitary needs of all 150 campers were served by a row of small toilet tents, each with a large bucket and clip-on toilet seat. It was the Senior Campers' ('Scampers') job to empty all twelve of these each morning, carrying the half-full (they certainly did not feel half empty!) five-gallon buckets of raw sewage, mixed with chemical disinfectant, across the field to tip them into the pit that had been dug by a JCB at a corner of the field specifically for the purpose.

We had the opportunity for a (nearly) dry run on the two mornings of the work party, but this did little to prepare me for the reality of the first morning after the campers had arrived and we were at full complement.

The task was so out of the ordinary that we simply had to get on and make the best of it with our team of six boys and six girls all aged 16 to 17. Once we had got over the shock of realising that this was our first duty as Scampers, we all dressed up in bin bags and marigolds and attacked the lat tents, passing their heavy buckets out of the little canvas door, then walking in a sideways human chain, each hand on a different lat-bucket, across the field, bathed in glorious Devon sunshine.

The most delicate part of the operation was the tipping of the contents into the pit. This was a highly skilled operation, if it was to be achieved without any back splash, which we almost mastered by the end of week one.

The Case of the Dirty Pants

All in all, the weeks flew by and we had an excellent team of Scampers that first year. The only shadow that started to darken the otherwise clear sky towards the end of the first week was the realisation that one of the lads in my team, and therefore in my tent, whom we'll call Jamie, had gone the entire first 5 days without changing his underwear!

His morning routine was to slip out of his boxers and into his underpants that had been kicked to the bottom of the sleeping bag the night before. An admittedly smooth operation that might be appropriate for a night or two, but this was not sustainable for the full 10 days and on Day 4 I made this very clear to him. When on Day 5 there was no change, the situation was, in my view, becoming unsafe. But Jamie was prepared to make no promises to reassure me.

Discussion and even threats had made no difference so I was forced into declaring an ultimatum. If he had not changed his base layer by the time we were due to do the lats the following morning I would be forced to take his sleeping bag and empty the contents into the lat pit, as I had no intention of reaching down into his sleeping bag to retrieve the contents by hand.

He acknowledged that he understood this but still did not agree to effect a change, so the following morning, as agreed, the entire line of Duty Scampers, lats in hand, made a detour via our tent to retrieve Jamie's sleeping bag, which I duly carried towards the lat pit. It was only when we were about half way across the field, lats and sleeping bag in hand that I started to feel that something just didn't add up.

I could understand why so many of the off-duty Scampers were following to watch the spectacle – the discussion, threats and final ultimatum were no secret amongst our team. I guessed they wanted to see if their rookie Scamper Leader would go through with his threat. But it was not until we were right beside the lat pit that I was able to put a finger on what was making me so uncomfortable. Foremost among the grinning Scampers, I noted, was Jamie himself. Why would he be finding this so amusing?

Once we had finished with the real job in hand, having laid aside the emptied, hosed and disinfected lat buckets, and washed our hands, I took Jamie's sleeping bag to the lat pit to lose the unsavoury contents into the contaminated hole in the ground. But the crowd of Scampers still seemed just a little too eager to see one of their own shamed in this way and the contents of this sleeping bag, I realised, felt just a little too heavy for just a pair of boxers. Maybe it would be worth a quick check before I held the sleeping bag open, out over the pit of disgust.

I have seldom made a wiser decision, as what had been in the sleeping bag on the triumphal procession across the field, much to all the Scamper's amusement, was not Jamie's boxers at all. These had been duly changed as requested, but there lying on the grass in their place were my jeans, my last pair of clean, dry trousers. And we still had 5 days of the holiday to go!

I learned a lot that week about leading young people. A dose of humour, tempered by a healthy portion of wary suspicion is often a good mix, especially as the relationship develops, people start to relax and the leeway for practical jokes opens wide. We wouldn't have it any other way though, would we?

One lesson for survival on a summer camp I had taken away from our time at Birch Bay Ranch came back to me at this point in the week, and it's a rule I have tried never to forget in this kind of youth work setting: 'You're never even, till you're one ahead!'

Marrying this cardinal rule of survival with Jesus' teaching about turning the other cheek is an acquired skill that I continue to try to perfect. I remain convinced it can be done!

A Second Visit to Salcombe

My first visit to Salcombe had happened during the summer before we had moved out of London. When the leaders' information pack came through for the following year, I was in no doubt that there could be no better use of my time than to return, this time with more experience under my belt as I had by now been trained as a kayak instructor.

Alan and Christine were generous enough to invite me to say a few words to the camp about what we were doing with Fair Glade Trust. This was to prove very significant as a number of leaders volunteered to help us with our own activity events as we got busier. Two guys in particular contacted us with a view to helping us on a longer term basis.

It was after our second summer at SU Salcombe that Tim, one of the climbing leaders, offered to move to Witney to help with our growing workload. A management accountant by training, Tim offered to take on the role of Company Secretary and look after our finances, along with assisting with any groups we might be invited to work with. This was a big step of faith for Tim and his fiancée Ruth, just when they were preparing to get married. They decided to make their first married home in Witney. In the weeks leading up to the wedding, Tim moved in to stay with us, whilst they looked for their first home.

It was a great encouragement to have someone else to work with, and Tim played a key role in helping set up our finances and working with our trustees as he was able to relieve Tessa of the duties of Company Secretary. Tim's support at this time was a huge God-send as Tessa was by now well into the responsibilities of full-time work as a solicitor, and starting to feel decidedly the worse for wear, as we realised she was expecting our first child!

No Fixed Abode

One of the key targets in our first months in Witney was to research suitable venues for the activities we wanted to offer, and ultimately, a fixed base for our adventure centre. This task would have been so much easier if we'd had a substantial reserve of cash to offer landowners in the area. Unfortunately we had none.

Many days were spent discovering local activity venues, including the places where we could access the River Thames for kayaking, and we even found a couple of bridges along the route of a disused railway line that we could use for abseiling. But any discussions about the possibility of something more permanent always faltered, understandably, over finance.

First Site?

It was shortly after I met with David Winter, vicar of the neighbouring village of Ducklington, and his wife Christine, that I received an unexpected invitation to an evening buffet at their home. They had invited a carefully selected group of local people who they thought would be interested in our embryonic local charity and might, in various ways, be in a position to help.

I was asked to make a presentation about our plans. This was to be followed by an opportunity to discuss as a group if there might be somewhere in the local area that would be suitable as an adventure centre, along with other ways that they might help.

One of the guests that evening was Andrew Townsend, owner of Standlake Sands and Gravels. He quietly invited me to get in touch with him some time over the next few days to arrange to meet up. When we met, he took me to visit the site of an exhausted gravel pit just north of the village of Standlake. As we walked round the 24 acres I was amazed to find that perfect mix of open flat ground, ideal for buildings and sports pitches, and woodland to hide our ropes course and climbing walls. It also had a fair-size (if a little choked up) lake, which would make a superb venue for introductory canoeing and kayaking. The parallels with the Birch Bay Ranch property were striking! To my amazement and delight, as we approached the perimeter of the land I found myself walking along the banks of the River Windrush!

So here was a site that would be ideal for our adventure centre, about 90 minutes' drive from Central London and bordering the River Windrush! Wow! But there remained the thorny issue of cost. How would we ever afford this large plot of land, with such potential, here in Oxfordshire?

'You can have it for £1,000 an acre,' Andrew said, 'and you can pay me as and when planning permission is obtained, which gives you time to raise the money and the assurance that you won't be paying for land until you are assured of planning permission!'

This was it then. Here was land that we would be able to afford, which would be ideal for our plans and which just happened to border on the River Windrush. All we needed to do now was prepare a suitable planning application and challenge our wonderful CLUB 111 supporters to get busy raising the £25,000 we'd need to buy the land.

Planning Permission

Everything looked set to go into hyperdrive. We had drawings made up of how we might use the land. David Mainse, a great encourager and inspiration to us, who had set up Circle Square Ranch, a wonderful chain of Adventure Ranches across Canada, even paid to send their design engineer Bill St Pierre across to help us come up with the best design for the land.

Armed with copious advice from both the planning department and a firm of local architects, we submitted our plans and waited on tenterhooks for the planning meeting that would decide the future of this land.

At the meeting itself we were hugely grateful for what turned out to be a very supportive committee and planning team. Consent was granted for an adventure centre and warden's house, pretty much exactly as we had requested. It seemed as if the biggest milestone on the way to setting up our adventure centre was achieved, and in a remarkable way.

With planning permission granted we set about clearing the site. We were delighted to show our supporters round this oasis in the Oxfordshire countryside, before issuing work gloves and inviting them to join us clearing scrap metal and other debris from the far end of the site. We then all retreated to Wycliffe Hall in Oxford where Andrew and Rachel Baughen, our good friends from London and co-founders of CLUB 111, hosted a summer barbecue and the not-too-official CLUB 111 AGM and prize-giving.

Roadblock

In the weeks that followed, with the help of a number of local volunteers, we cleared about four tons of rubbish from the site and the British Trust for Conservation Volunteers ran a hedge laying course for us. Everything seemed to be accelerating into a very exciting winter ahead. In the course of the last year, we'd successfully delivered our first school residential activity training courses; found a site and gained planning permission for it; I'd qualified in a number of outdoor activities; and to cap it all, we were expecting our first child in the autumn.

Then all of a sudden the rollercoaster hit a dramatic incline and seemed to grind to a gut-wrenching stop. We received notice that one end of the site for which we had just gained planning consent was the subject of a potential Compulsory Purchase Order so that a travellers' camp could be built in West Oxfordshire. We were told that there were twelve sites being considered, out of which only two were needed.

Since there were other possible locations, and the potential community benefits of our facility were plain to see, we were hopeful that the authorities would pick one of the other options for the site. All would be decided at a Public Enquiry to be held in the Council Offices in Witney in December.

We were advised to get a planning barrister to prepare our case. The period leading up to the birth of our first baby was therefore suddenly set against a backdrop of preparing for this hearing – a hearing which now seemed to have huge implications for the future of Fair Glade Trust in Oxfordshire.

12.

Good News and Bad News

The wonderful news was that our daughter Anna was born in Oxford on 10 November 1992, and all was well with both mother and daughter. The weeks immediately following this precious family time, however, were interrupted by numerous trips to London, preparing reams of written evidence about our planned use for the site and the bona fide nature of our organisation.

At the time, many kind local people reassured us that they had been praying and felt that the land would not be subject to compulsory purchase. My reply was always a little more circumspect: 'Please pray, not necessarily that we get the land, but that God's will be done – and that we only get the land if it is his will for our future with FGT.'

The public enquiry lasted five days, from 8–12 December, but the wait for the determination of the case seemed to take an age. It was not until well into the spring that we heard the news that of the twelve sites on offer, four acres of the land at Downs Road, Standlake had been selected for compulsory purchase by the Department of Environment Inspector.

Our trustees were therefore left with a choice. Press ahead with our plans on the remainder of the land and build our centre anyway, or to renew our search for another site in the area. Their strong sense was that since all the best building land had now been earmarked for purchase, and as there were now so many unknowns involved in pressing ahead, Fair Glade Trust should reluctantly inform Andrew that we were not able to proceed.

It seemed that our plans had ground to a halt. And we were left with some big questions, chief among them – where do we go from here? On the one hand, word was spreading about Fair Glade Trust in Oxfordshire, and the Public Enquiry had certainly raised our profile significantly in the area. On the other, we were now effectively an organisation that purported to deliver adventure activities, but with no fixed abode.

13.

When God Guides, God Provides!

When we moved to Witney, I had set up the Fair Glade Trust office in a spare room of our house. A second room was now occupied by Tim. It seemed there was nothing for it but to continue to develop the vision from our home, offering activities in the venues we had researched in the local area: on the river, from bridges and in local woods.

Working at home was a mixed blessing. It wasn't always easy for my 6-month-old daughter to understand why sometimes Dad was her best friend and at other times he was shutting himself away and not opening the door because he was working. When that inquisitive child became able to reach the ringing phone downstairs and then gurgle and dribble down the receiver – possibly to a teacher enquiring about a kayak session for their group or maybe even someone interested in supporting our work – it soon became clear that establishing and running an outdoor education charity from home might not be the best idea.

I was therefore immensely grateful to Glen Hocken, the discerning curate at St Mary's Cogges – the church we had decided to attend in Witney – who called me one day. When I had managed to wrestle the phone from our young receptionist, he mentioned that there were two vacant attic rooms above the church administrator's office, in the Old School House neighbouring the church. Perhaps we might like to relocate there?

I could immediately see the good sense behind this generous offer and arranged to meet Glen there as soon as we were both free. We climbed the single steep staircase to the tiny attic rooms, the only natural light coming from a small skylight set into the roof. It soon dawned on me that I was looking at the vacant first offices of the Fair Glade Trust.

The Volunteer Spirit

First impressions were that there was ample room for me as I would be working there alone for much of the time, in spite of the fact that the two roofs came in to meet each other at a steep angle from waist height, making it only possible to walk un-stooped down the middle three inches of each room, my hair brushing one side or other of the strip light.

Within a fortnight we had the phone connected and had moved our trusty Apple Macintosh and mono printer up into the new attic office. It was not long before we were taking a steady stream of calls requesting activity sessions or skills coaching from local scout groups and youth organisations.

It also wasn't long before the balance between being around to take the calls and being out preparing for and delivering sessions was getting hard to manage. It was therefore such an encouragement and amazing timing to pick up the phone one day and hear Anita, a young music student in our church, on the other end. She had just come back from university and wanted to offer to help out in the office with the ever growing administrative tasks, including manning the phone.

Another real boost came when we were joined by another of the climbing leaders from SU Salcombe. Peter Rowe offered his time to help get things off the ground, with the blessing of his wife, Kim, a trainee teacher at their local primary school in Coventry.

Thrown in at the Deep End

Soon after joining, Pete called with the exciting news that Kim's school was looking for a provider for their Year 6 residential and he had offered Fair Glade Trust's services. Apparently we were going to take them hiking, kayaking on the Thames, abseiling or climbing in the local area and offer a variety of team challenges – fully catered!

'What? But Pete, we're nowhere near ready!' I cried. 'We don't have anywhere to take them climbing or abseiling, or a minibus to transport the kids, not to mention boats for the kayaking. I am still not fully qualified to take groups out . . . and we don't have a chef.'

'Well Jon,' he calmly replied, 'we have to start some time and this is a great opportunity for us as the usual venue the school goes to is fully booked this year. We've got three months to sort it all. It'll be fine!'

In the event Pete was right, it all came together in some very unexpected and wonderful ways, and Parkgate School were clearly delighted as they went on to come back to us for the following five years.

The run up to their visit was not without its sleepless nights, however. There was a long list of things to be organised:

- finding a suitable site for the group to abseil, although this was tempered by my relief when I heard that my good friend and outdoor mentor, Graham, would be able to take the week off work to come and lead the abseiling;
- the need to find a suitable site to take the group onto the River Thames;
- the discovery that the centre we had booked near Oxford could not provide cutlery and crockery so we had to buy place settings for fifty, with money we did not have;
- the requirement to write up all the material for our activity programme, including a whole series of new team challenges and the material for our evening camp fire talks;
- the pressure that I now had to pass my kayak instructor assessment. It had already been booked prior to news of their visit, but failing was now not an option!

God's Provision . . . But Not as We Know It!

When people say, 'God works in mysterious ways,' there is one incident that immediately springs to mind, which makes it very hard for me to argue. Of all the preparations set in motion by Pete's phone call, the persistent and nagging awareness that we did not have a minibus, nor did we have the money to buy one, was one of the issues that seemed hardest to see a way around.

We had by now found a kind farmer who was happy for us to access the river with our kayaks across his field. After I visited the site and saw how boggy it could be, I decided that what we really needed was a 12-seater Land-Rover – an even more expensive proposition.

As the weeks ticked by and some of the other matters started to fall into place, not least passing my kayak instructor assessment at Islington Boat Club on a hard-frozen Grand Union Canal, the issue of the vehicle seemed to loom larger, and it became a frequent item for prayer at the time. The memory of it remains for me one of the most unlikely, yet clear examples of God's amazing provision: not necessarily what we wanted but exactly what was needed, right on time, and reliable. It all came together in a way that none of us could have expected!

One evening in semi-desperation I walked up to the petrol station at the top of our road and bought a copy of the *Thames Valley Auto Trader*. I am not sure why I decided to go out and pick up that magazine as we had no money to buy a Land Rover anyway. It was probably with a view to researching what was available and seeing how much they were selling for. When I turned to the relevant pages for 4x4s it did not take long to grasp the reality that we really could not afford anything in that section.

For some reason I then flicked back a few pages to the section of minibus listings. Again there was nothing we could afford, and some of the offerings looked decidedly dodgy and beat up. And yet the entry, three across and seven down on the page, a particularly scruffy looking minibus, caught my eye and held my attention.

For some reason I picked up the phone and called the contact number, just to ask a bit more about the vehicle. I was not interested in a minibus anyway – I wanted a Land Rover.

'Sorry mate,' said a voice. 'It's sold.'

'That's OK, thanks anyway,' I said. But for some reason I went on to tell him, 'I only wanted it to take kids canoeing, for a charity we're just setting up . . .'

'Take kids canoeing?' he interrupted. 'As it happens this used to be the minibus for the Great Britain Canoe Team, and the guy I sold it to is a friend of mine who only wants it for about 4 weeks to move some bricks around for a building job he's doing. Then he's going to sell it on . . .'

I couldn't believe what I was hearing. The man on the other end of the line continued. 'Why don't you give him a call and see if he'll sell it to you when he's done with it. He can't really ask much for it, because it looks pretty scrappy on the outside. It's been parked by the sea lots and had people climbing all over it to get boats off the roof, but I can tell you that the engine is sound. The BCU has had it serviced every year . . .'

What? Is this conversation really happening? It was beginning to feel like the impossible just might be possible!

He then gave me the number of his mate and told me to say he'd suggested I call. I phoned the guy as instructed and explained why we needed a bus, but all the while I couldn't help thinking, 'What if I'd picked any other minibus on that page to enquire about, or had decided to look in last week's edition or waited until next week?'

Meanwhile the 'man with the van' on the other end of the line was telling me that he still needed it for another 4 weeks, but after that . . .

'If it's for charity mate, you can bloomin' *'ave* it!'

I was stunned into silence. We've got a minibus! Eventually I managed to blurt out a bewildered 'thank you' before agreeing to call him again in 4 weeks' time to see how the building work was going, and arrange a date to pick it up.

In the event, it was about 6 weeks later and just before the school's visit, that I was given the whereabouts of the vehicle and a promise that although the owner would not be there on that day, it would be parked, unlocked, outside his house on a street somewhere in Richmond; the papers would be signed and under the passenger seat and the keys would be on the sun visor.

Ruth, Tim's wife to be, kindly agreed to drive me to Richmond to pick up our mystery-gift vehicle so I could drive it back. When we pulled up at the address there was the minibus as promised, complete with peeling Union Jack logos with the words 'Great Britain Canoe Team' on the back. The door was unlocked, the papers were on the passenger seat in full view and the keys were in the ignition!

Was this for real? Was it a stitch-up? I half expected to be arrested by pre-positioned police as I got in and started up the minibus. But when I got in and turned the key, it jolted into life first time and drove me back to Witney without a hitch. We had it serviced the next day and the following week it was towing our kayak trailer down to the river with excited children and two instructors, a journey it was to get to know well over the coming three years.

We never did get the Land Rover I had wanted, and in truth we could have done with a 4x4 on many an occasion on that riverside field, but whenever we did get stuck it happened that Nigel, a local sailing instructor and one of our early regular volunteers, always seemed to be on hand with his Fiat Panda 4x4 which did a superb job every time, much to Nigel's satisfaction, pulling our marooned Sherpa minibus out of the mud. Mysterious ways indeed!

'Let Him Have It!'

The provision of the kayaks and trailer was another detail that needed to fall into place and quickly! So perhaps I shouldn't have been surprised when a friend in North Wales called to alert us to the closure of an outdoor centre nearby that had announced their plan to sell off lots of their equipment, including a fleet of kayaks and a trailer, at a knock-down price.

But all this equipment and the vehicles needed to be stored somewhere and we certainly could not park them on the estate outside our front door. Once again David Winter's thoughtful invitation the previous year proved invaluable as Peter and Jane Boggis, who were guests that evening, had generously offered us the use of one of his barns to store any vehicles and trailers we might acquire.

The only awkward moment came when our church challenged David's to a friendly cricket match and I found myself bowling at Peter. David, by then a Fair Glade Trust trustee, and Peter's vicar, was umpire of the match. When I went to measure my run-up, before delivering my first ball at Peter, he put his arm out to stop me. He quietly advised me that it might not be prudent to bowl Peter out first ball. The chances of that happening were slim in any case, but I nodded sagely and sent two or three deliveries to one side or the other of the stumps, which the batsman successfully fended off.

The next over found Peter facing me again and the umpire's comment this time was something to the effect that it should be okay now to 'let him have it!' To David's amazement and mine too, I clean-bowled Peter with that very ball and he went off muttering something about wanting our vehicles and trailers out of his barn by Monday morning!

Help from Down Under

Meanwhile, Parkgate's school residential was fast approaching and the other big issue that had to be resolved was our need for a chef. I did not know anyone who would be free, not to mention up to the task, and I was most certainly not the right person to be cooking.

About one month before the visit I remembered Stewart Ross, my Aussie roommate in that crazy student house in Hampstead, about four years before. I wondered if he was still in London and still cooking so I dug out the address of my old student digs and wrote to him, in the hope he was still there.

It turned out that he had returned to Australia some time beforehand, and had been living there for the past two years, but had just come back to the UK and rented a room in our old house again! Yep he'd be happy to come and cook for us if I sent him the details.

And he did, for the next two years! What a wonderful servant heart! He was great with the kids, who liked his

Aussie accent and the international flavour it added to our team.

Stewart's Australian heritage also gave us a great basis for a theme for our camp fire session each evening. In honour of our Aussie chef, the first theme simply had to be 'Neighbours, everybody needs good neighbours' (to a well-known tune). This proved to be a superb topic for the first night away with the children, based on the Good Samaritan parable: 'Who do you think was the good neighbour to this man?'

This set the challenge for the week and for many school residentials to come – that their time together would only be truly successful if everyone was doing their bit to make sure everyone else in the group was happy. That's called being good neighbours.

There could only be one fitting option for our theme on the last night, again in honour of Stewart our Aussie chef, 'Home and Away'. What have we learned this week to take away with us as we go back home to our friends and family? How am I going to be different at home and at school as a result of my time away with my friends this week?

Encouraging Feedback

It is always good to hear feedback from groups who come to stay and this was particularly true after our first ever school residential, so we read with real interest the copies of the diaries the children had written when the school sent them on to us a couple of weeks after their visit.

One excerpt describing their first morning climbing and abseiling remains one of the more original diary entries we have ever received from a school, and gave us a real insight into the children's impressions of the adventures we had organised for them. (We have changed the names.)

Pete showed us how to put a harness on and safety things . . . Kuldeep went first. If you wanted to go up, you shouted 'climbing', and if you wanted them to tighten the rope you would say 'take in'. When Kuldeep was coming down it looked so easy and he said it felt great.

Then Gurmeena was coming down and I thought she was going to slip and had a fright but she never. She thought it was ace . . . We worked out a route for her and it worked a million. Sukhinder went next and you could tell she was doubtful. She nearly slipped at one point but quickly put her foot back on the ledge. Danielle was next and she was doubtful as well but done it.

It was me next and I thought it was brilliant and I felt quite proud when I'd done it. It didn't really scare me because when I was 7 I jumped out of my bedroom window and when I was 10 years old I fell through my grandma's garage roof and landed on my cousin!

It was of course, my good mate Graham Harris, who'd brought me out from London on numerous climbing and kayaking trips, who was running these abseiling sessions for us, while I took another group to the Thames in our ex-GB canoe team minibus!

We were delighted when it became clear that the staff at the school were very pleased with the trip and were planning to come back the following year. As I've said, they came back for the next five years and one of the teachers, who is now head of another primary school in Coventry, still brings his pupils back to us.

14.

Total Adventure and Sports*Plus*

As word began to spread about what we were offering, more and more groups were calling to arrange activity programmes.

One group I was particularly looking forward to welcoming back was the youth group from All Saints Brixton. Their leaders and I came up with a plan to offer a day's activities, which would then culminate in a simulated overnight 'drug squad' exercise. It began with a radioed-in request from local Special Branch to intercept a shipment of drugs, and the cash drop to pay for them.

In order to access their instructions and fulfil their mission, two different groups would need to abseil off a bridge, canoe down, then back up a river, and bike, off road, to specific locations. This meant that the skills learned during their activity days became very relevant as the exercise went long into the night.

Meanwhile, another group set about cracking codes and following clues to find a stash of emergency survival equipment on a piece of wild ground in the middle of nowhere (the gravel pit we had been offered near Standlake, before it was handed over for development).

As such an active day gave way to the evening we could not believe the conditions that unfolded. Temperatures during the week had plummeted sharply and snow was forecast. Eventually, the three groups came together at our gravel pit rendez-vous, by which time the emergency shelters had been put up, a fire lit and some well-earned hot chocolate was ready to serve. The glow on the kids' faces reflected the warming of our hands as we all roasted marshmallows on sticks.

It was a proud moment when Team A were able to deliver the bag of (self-raising) white powder, and Team B revealed a healthy stash of (foiled) gold coins, or was it ginger nuts? And everyone appreciated the roaring fire and emergency supplies of tents and hot food that had formed the third part of the exercise.

So 'Operation Golden Retriever' was born, a model we were to use on many occasions in the future with a wide variety of different groups.

Diet of Worms!

That spring I also had a call from a former US Marine who was now a church youth worker in Kingstanding, Birmingham. He wanted to bring a group of older teens who needed a real challenge and asked if he could come and use our wild site for some genuine survival work. His plan was to survive on the site for the weekend with the guys, utilizing whatever they could pick, snare or dig up. The menu was to consist of rabbit stew with wild garlic, nettle tea and a protein boost of shallow-fried worms, again flavoured with garlic.

I had no problem with them using the site but asked for written confirmation that it was entirely their own programme and FGT was in no way responsible for their activities or for the food hygiene! He was more than happy to sign up to this and was delighted just to have found a piece of waste ground that he could access legally with his group.

I deliberately stayed away during the day but decided to go down to check they were all okay on the Saturday evening. I eventually found them deep in the woods, all sitting round a camp fire with a frying pan just off to the side. They looked genuinely distraught when I appeared in the circle of light thrown out by the fire: 'Oh sorry Jon, we didn't know you were coming. We've just finished the last of the worms!'

They kindly offered to dig me up some more, but I thought they looked tired after a hard day's surviving, and naturally did not want to put them to the extra work!

A Growing Family

So things picked up with growing momentum and the next couple of years saw us working with an ever-growing number of groups, from a variety of locations around Oxfordshire. By now we were also making the occasional sortie with local groups into the Forest of Dean, 90 minutes to the west of us.

I continued to train towards a number of other qualifications including BETA (the Basic Expedition Training Award – now BEL) and gaining experience in rock climbing, white-water canoeing and sea kayaking.

The support from CLUB 111 was an ongoing encouragement for us both and helped sustain FGT in those early days. By the summer of 1993, we had over eighty members and at our CLUB 111 AGM were delighted to be able to announce that our members, organised so capably by Andrew and Rachel Baughen, had raised over £3,800 towards the now growing work of FGT.

Meanwhile, on the home front, family life continued to be equally absorbing and it was not long before we were able to announce the seasonal news, just after Christmas, of the birth of a baby boy. Murray Jon was born, eventually, much to Tessa's relief, on 23 January 1994, bringing our family total to four.

Yet another special person to journey with us and bring encouragement in the midst of our shared 'adventure of faith'.

A Developing Partnership

Our friendship with Steve and Michelle Connor of Christians in Sport (CIS) was another rich source of encouragement to us. Indeed, it was during a meeting with Steve, held in a canoe on the sun-drenched River Cherwell, that we decided to explore the idea of working together on a summer camp.

Christians in Sport were not at that time running any sports camps for young people. I had had it on our agenda since the inception of FGT to offer summer camps. When I mentioned it to Steve we could both see huge potential for encouraging young sports enthusiasts through such events.

So it was that we hit on the plan of approaching Coke-thorpe School once again, this time to ask if they would be prepared to host the first Total Adventure Holiday for FGT, and the first Sports*Plus* camp for Christians in Sport, in the summer of 1994. When the Trustees of FGT and the board at CIS both approved the plan, and Cokethorpe came back to say they would be happy to welcome us, it was time to get the word out.

Steve offered to be the speaker for the Sports*Plus* week and I agreed to speak at Total Adventure. We would offer a split programme of sports, organised by CIS, and adventure activities organised by FGT – including archery, air riflery, kayaking, canoeing and climbing. With this decision to develop Total Adventure Holidays Sports*Plus* camps it was as if someone had fired the starting gun and the race was on to prepare for the summer.

'That's Not How You Do It, Jon!'

Cokethorpe was a fantastic setting for our sports and adventure holidays, with acres of sports fields, including two lovely grass tennis courts. A local farmer had generously given us permission to canoe on one of his lakes and the chapel in the grounds was an ideal venue for our evening Roadshow.

The only facility that was lacking was somewhere to take the campers climbing. The solution, inspired by our experience at Birch Bay Ranch, was to build a climbing and abseiling tower in the woods at the back of the school – with the school's permission of course! Having no experience of building any structures, let alone a specialist climbing tower, we found ourselves on yet another steep learning curve. Someone put me in touch with a good friend who had a small business making resin-coated climbing panels and a selection of climbing holds. We also discovered that a member of our local church congregation was regional manager for a national scaffolding company. He was able to advise us on the design of a suitable tower and arrange for delivery at a charitable rate.

Even with these welcome developments, there were one or two challenges still to overcome. For example, we were keen to follow accepted guidelines for the construction of the wall. However, since most scaffolding structures are temporary and many are attached to permanent buildings, there were no national approved guidelines for free-standing, permanent scaffolding structures. We therefore decided to build it to comply with standard good practice, and then set it in a foundation of six tons of concrete!

A local JCB driver was generous enough to dig a square pit of the right dimensions – yet another example of the many ways in which God provided, some in answer to spoken prayers, others just a helping hand from the Father as he watched his children trying to go where he called them.

I should not give the impression that it was all plain sailing however. There was a moment of minor panic when the headmaster, who had been so encouraging throughout, appeared looking very cross, complaining about the arrival of a large articulated lorry at the edge of his garden.

'How exactly are you planning to get the scaffolding from the school drive, to the woods where you plan to position the climbing wall?' he demanded.

Apparently he had already been surprised once that day, when he had looked out from his study to see a JCB operator driving across his pristine lawn! We agreed to have the scaffolding unloaded where it was and then carry all the poles to the site of the proposed wall. This may have sounded like a simple solution, although it represented another evening of hard labour for me and two volunteers, but there was no alternative to getting the 6-ton cement mixer booked for the following week.

I enlisted the help of a couple of local volunteers and my 14-year-old nephew from Gibraltar, Christian, who was staying with us. We worked pretty much round the clock to get the scaffolding up in time for the cement mixer to come and pour the concrete foundation a week later. It was a late finish the night before, but by dusk we had just put in the uppermost horizontals, which were to be the anchor point for the abseil.

The next morning dawned, once again bright and dry, and Pete, Christian and I gathered together a motley collection of spades and shovels and headed down to the new scaffold tower to meet the cement mixer at 8 a.m. It was with some relief that I guided the driver of this diesel-powered dinosaur through the otherwise quiet woodland, along our specially prepared track, to our new 30-foot-high wall, gleaming in the morning sun.

As the driver reversed up to our precision dug square pit, we readied ourselves to start spreading the concrete. Nothing had prepared me for the seemingly endless quantity of semi-turgid gunge that spewed out of the back of that truck when the driver pulled the lever.

Our job was simple, to smooth out the concrete with our spades and shovels, but it soon became clear that these tools in our inexperienced hands were no match for the unstoppable quantities which continued to gush into our pit. It was vital to get the top of the apron absolutely flat and level before it went off. Any dents or unevenness left in the surface of the concrete would forever be the spot where puddles would form and leave slippery and unsightly areas of green slime, and if these were located around one of the many scaffolding uprights, they would soon become a focus for premature weathering and rust.

Once the driver had delivered his load, he closed up the back of the mixer and drove away leaving us to work in the growing heat to try and level out the newly poured concrete apron before it went off. Before long it became clear that it was firming up more quickly than we could cope with, not least because it was so hard to judge if an area was actually flat or not.

I was starting to despair and dread the prospect of an uneven, puddling surface for years to come when a voice rang out in a broad Essex accent from out of the undergrowth to the side of the wall.

'That's not how you do it, Jon! Here take the end of this!' There stood Hudson Owen, the windsurf leader from Salcombe!

'What is he doing here?' I thought. I hadn't seen Hud for over two years and now he had materialised out of nowhere, offering me the other end of a scaffold board, grinning, but looking like he meant it.

There was no time to stop and argue as the concrete continued to harden in the July sunshine. I put down the shovel and grabbed hold of one end of the board. We squatted down and patted the edge of the board across the surface of the concrete until the whole thing was completely flat. Job done! With the concrete surface going off fast, and now completely level under the midday sun, there was time for a welcome hug and catch up with Hud – and of course an explanation as to how he had appeared out of the undergrowth, just when we needed his help.

I was amazed to hear that he had just come back from a gap year in Uganda with Tear Fund. As an engineering student, he had been building roads for the past six months in the baking East African heat. He knew all about levelling tarmac before it went off too quickly, and he just happened to show up at our house that morning to visit us.

Tessa had told Hud where he would find us, and the engineer in him was only too keen to see how we'd approached building a climbing wall. My expertise, as he well remembered, lay more in the latrine department! Yet another God-incidence, as David Winter, by then one of our Trustees, would call it.

We Made It!

Building a climbing wall was only one aspect of preparing for our first multi-activity holiday for children and our first joint venture with Sports*Plus*. The list of other preparations seemed unending, and at times it felt like we'd never be ready.

We'd need a team that was larger than ever before, including dormitory leaders, activity instructors, cooks, drivers and musicians. We also had to produce a whole ream of risk assessments to cater for new activities and issues related to taking care of individual children, as opposed to working with a group and their leaders.

Dorm plans, rooming lists, activity timetables, menus, ingredients and shopping lists, arts and crafts materials, music and musicians, PA, lighting, vehicle hire and insuring approved drivers, checking qualifications of new team members, booking arrangements with the school (including marrying up our two insurance policies to check there were no gaps), acquiring bought and borrowed activity kit, arranging access and permissions to activity venues, advertising the holidays, briefing the speakers and writing dorm leaders' notes, child protection training, safety training, rotas for washing up, rotas for dorm patrol, rotas for morning thoughts, rotas for activity sessions, a briefing for the camp nurse and medication administration charts – these were just some of the jobs that needed to be organised.

Every day was long and jam-packed with the deadlines of information to get out to parents and volunteers, not to mention the food or equipment to order. There were days in the lead up to that first Total Adventure Holiday when I did not switch the computer off until after three in the morning.

The days leading up to our first week of Total Adventure passed in a blur of activity but I will never forget that feeling of sheer relief when finally all the kids were booked in, breakfasted and heading off for their first activity sessions. We had managed to attract a healthy number of children to our first ever Total Adventure and all the team positions were filled. We had completed a positive team training and all the activities were set up and waiting.

I looked out of the window to see one of the minibuses driving off with Drew at the wheel, a very experienced kayak instructor I'd met during my visits to Scotland. 'We made it,' I thought. All the kids were out on properly risk-assessed activities, with qualified instructors, at superb activity venues, including our very own climbing wall.

'Phew!'

'Sam's Been Shot!'

I was about to turn my attention to organising the dorm lists and staffing for the following week when I heard the rushing feet of one of our campers on the steps outside my room:

'Jon, Jon, you'd better come quickly. Sam's been shot in the eye, at air riflery!'

'Whaaaat?' 'Noooooooooooo?'

Surely not! It seemed as though all the efforts of the previous few months had been shot to pieces, literally, right at the start of the very first activity session.

I left my desk at a run and followed the energetic but unwelcome messenger to see for myself. As I ran round to the rifle range, images flashed through my head of a young camper in his Total Adventure tee shirt and shorts, with his eye covered in blood, or even hanging out.

I arrived at the range in an instant and burst in on what I found to be an unnervingly calm atmosphere.

'Where's Sam? Is he blind? Is he bleeding badly?'

'Hey? Oh no, he's fine!' came the reply from our trained and appropriately qualified activity leader. 'He's fine – but he did get a tiny cut to his eyebrow!'

The .177 air rifles we were using were equipped with telescopic lenses and although he'd been advised not to, Sam had put his eyebrow right up to the near end of the lens, so when he pulled the trigger on his first shot, the kickback had knocked the rifle sight back onto his eyebrow, causing the smallest of grazes.

Same Time Next Year

It was with some relief that I looked back later on our first summer camps, when escaping to Brittany for our family holiday at the end of the summer. Our plan, modelled on the Birch Bay Ranch approach, had been to give the kids such a brilliant time that they would want to come back next year, and eventually to come back as leaders when they were old enough.

If we could achieve this, then we would genuinely be offering a strong incentive to our campers to keep making positive decisions throughout their teenage years. All the indicators were that we could not have got off to a better start. Not only had the week had an unblemished safety record, apart from a few headaches from too much exercise in the sun and one swollen eyebrow, but all the initial feedback indicated the kids had really enjoyed it and would definitely be back next year.

15.

Team Building

With the plan to make Total Adventure a regular fixture, a booking already made for Parkgate School to come back to us the following year, and the telephone ringing with more and more requests for our services, things were starting to get hectic.

Pete and Tim had now moved on to pursue their respective careers in engineering and management accounting, so it really was down to me to be there for every request for FGT's services, and to ensure we could deliver the agreed range of activities with the help of a growing team of volunteers. This was a challenge to say the least.

With all the added activity at home, now with two children below the age of 3, and at FGT, it was becoming clear that we needed help.

Earlier in the summer, in the midst of those hectic days leading up to the first week of Total Adventure, I had seen an advert in the CCI (Association of Christian residential and outdoor centres) magazine: 'Professional couple looking to move back to the UK to help a Christian residential ministry get established.' Even though I had been absolutely swamped by the workload of pulling together our first Total Adventure event, I knew that I had to make time to follow this up. So I contacted Mac and Jan Dick, who were at that time living in Voorschoten, Holland. In the very week leading up to that first TA, they had written back asking for more information about our work and how we saw it growing. I had no time to reply, yet I knew it was too important not to.

With that first hectic summer now a memory, Mac and Jan got back in touch in the autumn and invited me to the Netherlands to meet them. They generously offered to cover the cost of the flight and invited me to stay in their home for the weekend.

First impressions from my end were of a generous, fun-loving couple, committed to the English Speaking Church in the Netherlands, and to the youth group there. I also glimpsed, particularly in Mac, a sense of humour that would ensure a working relationship would never get stale or boring.

By the end of the weekend we had eaten well, visited their church, met a number of their friends, and talked and talked. They asked questions about life in Witney, my family and where we were at in developing the work of FGT. I was impressed by their desire to explore where God wanted them to commit their energies as they took early retirement and planned to move back to the UK. Looking back on it, I am not sure who was interviewing who, but it was certainly a great opportunity to begin to get to know each other. We parted at Schiphol airport with a plan to meet up when they were next in the UK.

I was very aware that they offered a unique opportunity to move FGT on to a new level. Mac's background in business, and as a Chartered Accountant, combined with his irrepressible good humour and commitment to young people and to God, would make him the perfect business partner and companion in what had felt like an unexpectedly lonely journey, even though there were people around all the time.

I could already see how refreshing it would be to have the help and support of a colleague to share ideas with, not to mention someone who could take on some of the work load. Better still, Jan was offering to support our work in the office, with secretarial and admin support . . . *and* she was a qualified counsellor!

An Important Visit

Later that Autumn, Mac and Jan got back in touch to say they were planning a trip to the UK and wondered if they might come and meet Tessa and the family and visit the FGT office. They made it clear that they also had at least one other centre to visit, with whom they were also exploring a future placement. I made every effort to clear the debris that had already accumulated in our attic office and we brought two more chairs up the narrow stairs so we'd all have somewhere to sit.

The day of their visit to Witney arrived and we were pleased to welcome them to our home. I knew they would take to Tessa and the kids, and that Tessa would immediately warm to them, which made it even more crucial that the visit to our tiny loft office, where Anita and I worked from a single computer and answerphone, did not put them off.

As we climbed the steep stairs and emerged to see the angled ceilings, with peeling, patchy wallpaper, closing in from both sides, I knew that wherever their other visit took them, it had to represent a more attractive opportunity than working up here day after day. I sat down to switch on the computer so Mac could have a look at our systems, such as they were. He then asked to see our accounts, and I was so grateful for Tim's hard work and professional approach to our last year-end.

We spent some time chatting about the roles they might each play if they came to join us. When it was nearly time to say our farewells, I was almost lost for words as I tried to describe some positive aspects to a possible future here in Oxfordshire. We'd been shuffling around each other, under those sloping ceilings, trying to find room for us all to sit down! As we parted, I shared what was on my mind.

'I have no idea what other positions you are exploring during your UK visit, and I can't deny that this office does not represent the most enticing of settings for your next move,' (especially true, I thought, when seen in contrast to the multi-million dollar manufacturing plant where Mac was currently MD) 'but one thing I am sure of: the other organisation you are going to visit will already have at least some of the expertise that you bring; whereas, if you come here, every single aspect of your experience and training will bring new skills and experience to FGT, and will make a huge difference.'

It may not have been an offer of mega bucks or future glamour, but there was no denying the truth of the claim, or the extent of our need.

Red Letter Day

Wednesday 15 February 1995 was a red letter day in the history of FGT because it was the day Mac and Jan joined the team. We received the encouraging news that they had decided to throw in their lot with us some weeks before and they had been over to view properties on a couple of occasions. By February they had moved over, moved in and were ready to start work.

This signalled a new era for FGT as we had just tripled the size of our full-time team, which meant we had to get organised with employment contracts, employee insurance and other key steps in building an organisation.

It will not be easy to erase from the memory, the 'unconventional' meeting with the senior partner of Tessa's former legal firm – Mr Ian Welch, of John Welch and Stammers – who had kindly offered to help us draft our first contracts. Although Tessa had worked with him for just under two years, I had only met him on a couple of occasions and was aware that this was one occasion when I ought to behave myself and try to elevate the credibility of FGT. But the conversation seemed to have ideas of its own.

'OK, so your new employee's name is . . .'

'Mac Dick'

'Is that with an M A C or an M and little c?'

'Sorry?'

'Do you spell his name MacDick or McDick. M A C or an M and little c?'

'Oh I see. No, his name is Mac . . . Dick. His first name is Malcolm . . .'

'Right, so his name is Malcolm McDick. I was simply asking if you spell that with an M A C or Mc?'

We did, eventually get past the first question, but it was clear to me we had not got this meeting off to a great start.

However, it was when we came to discuss the salary we had agreed to pay Malcolm Dick, FCA, that the conversation really went off the rails.

Knowing the fragility of FGT finances at the time, Mac had generously offered to come and work for a fraction of what someone with Mac's qualifications and experience could expect, and I don't think Jan asked for a salary at all.

When I answered Mr Welch's question about Mac's salary, his eyebrows shot up, then settled, as an assumed understanding dawned.

'So what is that per year?' he asked.

I repeated the same figure and he fixed me with a steady look.

'Do you mean to tell me that is his annual salary and not what he will be paid each month?'

'Erm, yes,' I nodded.

'Is Malcolm aware of this?'

I felt somehow ashamed when I nodded my confirmation, feeling very like the schoolboy in the headmaster's study being told he could do better. When the meeting finally drew to a close, we thanked Ian for giving his time to assist us in drafting our first employment contract. I am not sure if he'd been impressed with the depth of support and generosity evident in Mac's agreed terms of employment, or if he just thought we were all completely off the wall.

A Challenging Stay

Our work continued to accelerate and with Mac and Jan on the team we were able to accommodate more requests to work with a growing number of guests. Plus there was the encouragement of being able to share ideas, concerns and the vision.

Mac was keen to grow his experience in the outdoors and we discussed how best to go about this. I suggested that it would be a very steep curve to try to master all of the activities we offered at once, so he should focus his efforts on one main sport initially, and go for it.

It was shortly after his first experience kayaking with me (with a school group in a freak blizzard, upside-down for at least some of the time) that Mac told me he had chosen sailing as his preferred activity! So began a working relationship that was to bring us into contact with a wide variety of groups, at centres across the south of England.

Our first residential experience together was with a group from Cheltenham. Cheltenham is not renowned for its large urban ghettos and problems of delinquency. However, the leaders informed us that the estate the young people were from had recently recorded the highest petty crime rate in the UK.

We had planned quite a challenging activity week for this group including a long walk on the first day, canoeing on Symonds Yat and some rock climbing. The first activity, however, was the evening meal soon after they arrived. The noise level was running quite high in the dining room as the fifteen young people waited for the food to be served. The situation was not helped by the youth leaders shouting for the youngsters to be quiet which, of course, only increased the noise level further. The eventual solution was an ear-splitting referee's whistle.

This naturally made the cacophonous noise level in the crowded, uncarpeted, echoing dining room, almost unbearable.

I caught Mac's eye and wondered how he was finding his first experience of youth residentials with FGT. At this point the group leaders came to me and asked me to go with them out of the room to discuss taking the group straight home as they were clearly unmanageable. They should never have come!

'But we haven't even started yet,' I replied. 'The whole point of bringing them away is to give them new experiences and help them to see, through the way they respond to challenges, that they each have a positive contribution to make in different situations, and to help build their self-esteem. If we take them home now, we'll all have failed, before we've even started.'

We agreed to weather the storm for one day and see how the group was shaping up by the following evening.

The next morning dawned with a clear sky and the promise of a beautiful day ahead. We had programmed in quite a long walk: being dropped by the River Wye near Tintern Abbey and walking back through the forest. I was not sure how the group would cope with this long trek for their first activity, but once we were out and dropped off, there was only one way back, on foot.

All the leaders were fully expecting a day of grumbling and shuffling of feet. I had little doubt that the exercise would be greatly helped by the beauty that surrounded us: a combination of views through the trees of the river beneath and impressive cliffs above us, the constant, quiet noises of the woodland all around and the forest fragrances of conifers in the sun.

But we were some miles out with a long walk ahead of us, when the minibus drove off. How would the day shape up with this restless group of urban teens? Apart from one or two in the group who genuinely found such a walk a strain on the system, there was a discernible mellowing in atmosphere amongst the group as a whole and by that evening the leaders were persuaded it was definitely worth staying on to see how the week would shape up.

The following 2 days offered a combination of climbing and abseiling on the crags at Symonds Yat, and canoeing down the River Wye, on the flat water and the rapids. The group really got into these adventures and as we shared more experiences together, we witnessed first-hand how effective these activities could be in building relationships with young people with whom we would otherwise have very little in common.

It was great to see how after a day on the river, young people and their leaders, including our FGT team, were now sitting at the same tables, with so much to talk about. But the real test would come on the last day, a day of team building within the grounds of The Woodcroft Centre, where we were staying. In amongst the exercises on offer were a number of tasks which, if we'd asked the guys to do them on the first day they would simply have laughed, or walked away – or worse. These included, for one team, cleaning the inside, for another, washing the outside of both minibuses, and for the third, packing the buses so we were ready to leave after lunch.

By the end of the morning our old blue minibus had never been cleaner since we had been given it, nor would the interiors ever be as spotless again until she eventually retired. The fun the kids had whilst working on it was great to see. They had really learned to trust each other, work together and to enjoy the benefits of teamwork and friendship. And we had seen, perhaps for the first time, the efficacy of this approach to 'adventure youth work'.

Yellow Braces

Shortly after Mac and Jan joined the team, we were asked to provide activities for 'Yellow Braces', a packed programme of activities for young people laid on by the Diocese of Oxford Youth Advisor. In addition to providing canoeing and climbing, I was asked to be the speaker for a workshop on prayer.

We had just managed to obtain a grant to purchase our first ever brand new Old Town canoes. As I was running the canoeing session during that afternoon, once again from our friendly farmer's field on the Thames, we decided to test our new canoes to see how many people we could fit in one before it would actually sink! The total was impressive: 19 in all, mostly children with a couple of adults.

All was going well and there was a lot of laughter until one of the kids decided to rock the boat – literally! With that many people in a boat, there was very little freeboard, which is the height of the boat above the water level, so the slightest rock resulted in the canoe taking on water, which meant it sank a little lower, leaving even less freeboard. Laugher turned to hysterical screams.

Suitably encouraged, the lad rocked the boat again. Before long we were all in the water, which was not a problem on this sunny afternoon in a sheltered inlet of the river, until one girl started to gasp,

'Aah! My breathe-box! My breathe-box! I can't breathe! I can't breathe!'

Assuming she meant her inhaler, which she had not declared she had needed, we stopped fooling around and got her straight out onto the bank and to safety. At which point I asked her where her inhaler was.

'My what?' came her puzzled reply – by now she'd totally calmed down.

'Your inhaler; your breathe-box! Where is it?' I asked again.

'Oh, nah! I don't have one of them! It was my Reeboks, my new Reeboks. They was getting wet!'

He Who Refreshes Others, Will Himself Be Refreshed

There are so many more stories that could be told, but the bigger picture for Tessa and me at this time was the massive encouragement we felt in having a couple like Mac and Jan join us for the long term, to help put FGT on a more business-like footing. I am not sure what Mac thought of his new colleague but I found him to be a fantastic support, both in the office and on so many varied group bookings.

In the background he worked to develop our accounting and management structures whilst developing his skills as a sailing instructor and it was not long before he achieved the high accolade of being an RYA Senior Instructor and Power-boat Instructor.

Truly the team was coming together.

16.

A 'Qualified' Success

For me, 1995 was a key year for further training in outdoor skills. Mountain Leader Training in the spring only served to teach me how much more I had to learn. This prompted several sorties to Snowdonia and the Brecon Beacons with friends like Graham or Luke, a local volunteer we'd got to know in Witney, to work on navigation and camp craft.

We would typically set off after work on a Friday evening and arrive well into the night, park the car and stride off into the darkness, usually up a steep mountain path, in search of a suitable place to pitch a tent. Sometimes we'd wake up to beautiful views of the National Park. At other times we would emerge from the tent into thick fog or sheeting rain. We would cook breakfast on our Trangia® stoves and set out on our pre-planned route.

There were times when, after a busy week, the last thing any of us wanted to do was drive for 4 hours on a Friday evening and pitch a tent in the dark somewhere up a steep and rocky path.

Sometimes I remember packing for these trips with the beginnings of flu or a sore throat and head cold. The sensible thing to do in such a situation would be to call the trip off. But the lesson I learned was that invariably, however rough I'd felt leaving home on the Friday night, by the Sunday evening I came back feeling not only much better, but absolutely refreshed and revitalised. I know that if I'd followed the sensible advice and stayed at home, taking paracetamol, sipping hot lemon and honey drinks and lounging in long hot baths, I'd still have been feeling under the weather on Monday.

The Chattanooga Choo Choo?

By the autumn of 1995 Luke and I felt ready to present ourselves for our Mountain Leader Assessment at Oxfordshire's Outdoor Education Centre in Glasbury-on-Wye. This involved subjecting ourselves to 5 days of scrutiny – the first 2 days heading out from the centre to test our skills in navigation and 'security on steep ground', before leaving for an expedition over 2 nights and 3 days.

Our assessors were Martin and Ian. Martin was one of the full-time staff at the centre, with a reputation for not being the easiest assessor, and Ian was Head of Centre and the Chair of the Mountain Leader Training Board. It was evident from the start that this was going to be no walk in the park.

During the first 2 days we had some interesting exercises to tease our brains. When out walking on such a training or assessment, each candidate is often asked to lead a short section, or 'leg', to find a clearly defined feature such as a stream junction, small crag or sheepfold.

My two tasks on that first day were to try and locate a lake (that didn't actually exist) and a ring contour, which you can normally expect to see as you approach it, because it usually takes the form of a nobble of raised ground.

On this occasion, however, the assessor had thoughtfully chosen a shake-hole, or sharply depressed dip, caused by an underground cave that had collapsed centuries ago. The result was that it showed no evidence of the change in elevation you would normally expect, as you approach a ring contour from a distance, leaving the student on assessment with the very disconcerting feeling of leading the team, including his assessor, towards an area of raised ground that patently was not there.

The main part of the Assessment which was to follow, was the 3-day expedition in Snowdonia. On this extended trip, the assessor could turn to any one of the candidates at any time and ask any question: about the natural environment, what the weather was likely to do or how he or she would respond to a particular scenario. Frequently they would ask a candidate to pin-point their exact location and justify their position.

Our expedition took us on a very interesting route up one side of Crib Goch, a renowned steep-sided rocky ridge to the east of Snowdon, and down the other. Suddenly, Ian, our assessor turned to look down from his position just above me on what felt like a near-vertical ascent.

'Jon, what pulls into Baltimore about a quarter to four?'

'Pardon?' Surely I must have misheard him, as we clung to the side of the mountain, his voice trailing off into the wind as it whistled up the side of the arête all around us.

'*What pulls into Baltimore about a quarter to four?*' he shouted.

I assumed Ian's question must be referring to some safety technique I had never heard of, so I was left with no alternative but to reply,

'Sorry Ian I have no idea!'

He looked down and replied matter-of-factly, 'The Chatta-nooga Choo Choo!' He gave me a broad grin and continued his ascent above me.

'What on earth was that about?' I thought as I waited for his foot to move up and away, to vacate my next hand hold. Later I came to realise that as mountain leaders, we'd need the ability to feel sufficiently at home in this very steep environment to engage in conversations about other topics, not just survival. I might, after all, next time be leading a group in this environment myself, if successful, and then I'd certainly need to be able to think of other's needs and not be totally absorbed in my own route planning.

Cold Socks and Red Shrikes

The next day I found myself the subject of another of Ian's ruses, or perhaps more accurately, he rumbled one of mine.

I was walking along as part of the group, taking a bit of time to relax as one of the other candidates led his leg of the journey, when Ian turned to me with two questions in quick succession.

Pointing to a mountain in the middle distance he asked me what it was called. I could not mistake the rounded shoulder of Moel Siabod, remembering the night spent up there with Graham and Luke some months before. It was particularly memorable because when I went to put my walking socks on, the morning after a particularly cold night, I found them frozen rigid.

He then pointed to a small bird, about the size and colour of a sparrow that had just darted out from the heather in front of us and asked me what it was. I had used my BSc in Environmental Sciences to focus on issues of desertification in Sub-Saharan Africa, so it was no good to me here and I had absolutely no idea. Of course I answered confidently, nonetheless: 'That, Ian, is a red shrike!'

Ian looked visibly impressed and we strode on. Boosted in confidence, I decided to milk the one unit from my degree course relevant in this situation and started to expand upon the various different mushrooms we saw, stating which should be avoided and which could probably be eaten safely (though I'm not sure I'd ever have put this to the test).

It was not until about six hours later when we'd arrived at our agreed camp site, the tent was up and I was hunched over the stove cooking my evening meal, that I became aware of my assessor's walking boots standing very close by. I looked up and followed Ian's gaze on up into the sky to a large buzzard circling high above.

He then looked down at me and asked, rhetorically: 'Another red shrike, Jonathan?'

I had no defence, but again answered confidently, trying not to sound too cheeky, 'No Ian, I think you'll find that is a buzzard!'

I have to say that of all the entry-level assessments I have endured, the Summer Mountain Leader Assessment was the most arduous, and comprehensive, but also the most enjoyable and I am sure it is one of the easiest not to pass first time!

I was relieved to see on my report at the end of the assessment a comment from Ian: 'A strong performance, but the candidate needs to brush up on his knowledge of Glen Miller songs!'

Ian was too statesmanlike to refer to my dire knowledge of mountain bird life, but when I later consulted a colourful volume on our book shelves at home, *The Birds of Britain and Europe*, I was dismayed to find there is no such bird as a red shrike, only a red-*backed* shrike!

Tight Eddies

This humiliation was surpassed substantially, however, by an experience on my five-star kayak assessment, part of which took place on the River Tryweryn, in North Wales.

My assessor's job was to test my river reading and boat positioning skills. At five-star level, which is the top award of technical competence, the view of the assessors is simple. If they would be happy to paddle a particular stretch of river, or put their boat in a particularly munchy wave, then we, as potential five-star paddlers, should be confident too.

Being one of the top paddlers in the country, the assessor gave me one task: 'Follow where I go. I'm going to make some pretty tight eddies. If you manage to paddle a similar line to me, then we can probably assume you are paddling at the right level.'

So we set off down the boulder section known as the graveyard, with Loel, my assessor, taking every eddy and working the river hard. It was when he turned to me just above the 'ski jump', a long shoot of water that ends in a maelstrom at its base (which you would not want to drop into sideways), he said to me, 'I am going to make the micro-eddy halfway down on the right. When I come out of it, you set off and see if you can make it too.'

This wasn't the first time I had paddled this river and I had often seen top paddlers make this tiny eddy but never wanted to risk it myself because missing it would mean a very untidy descent into what lay beneath. I was acutely aware too that my Diablo craft was quite a bit longer at the front than his short stubby Vertigo play boat, which would only make it harder to spin the boat successfully into the tiny eddy.

Ah well, now was the time to make it work. As I crossed the lip of the ski jump, I felt gravity pulling me down towards the base of the ramp. I pointed the boat hard to the right, aiming for just above the micro-eddy to give time to turn the boat, in the hope that the still water in the eddy would catch the boat and hold me there.

To my amazement and relief I found myself sitting securely in the eddy I had only ever watched others go for. Then I managed to break back into the fast flow of water as it shot down to the base of the ski jump and made it across to the far side of the river in time to catch the eddy to the left of the frothy munchy 'hole' that spanned the bottom of this real life wild waterslide.

Tighter Toilets

By lunch time, things seemed to be going well, and Loel suggested we take a break in the café conveniently situated halfway down the river. It was at this point that my life began to unravel. I decided to take the opportunity for a comfort break, a rare luxury halfway down a white-water river, and found an empty cubicle in the gents.

The combination of a damp backside from sitting in a white-water kayak, and a broken toilet seat, soon resulted in me sliding right off the side of the toilet, wedging myself, and the detached toilet seat, firmly in the narrow gap between the porcelain and the cubicle wall, elbows squashed up against my ears!

This would be embarrassing enough in any circumstance but the thought of getting found in this predicament on my five-star white-water kayak assessment was too farcical to contemplate.

I could already hear my assessors' comments to his mates over a beer in the bar that evening, and probably for months or years to come: 'White-water kayak leader? He couldn't even be trusted to sit on a toilet without falling off!'

It was at this point that the door to the Gents creaked open and I instantly recognised the wetsuit boots of my assessor entering the room and standing at the urinal, just inches from where I was sitting at his feet, separated thankfully by the cubicle panel.

I had to sit there in absolute silence while he went about his business, washed his hands, dried them and left the room, before wresting myself from the ridiculous predicament I had now wedged even more securely into, and up off the floor!

'Right,' I said to myself, trying to collect my thoughts as I finally left the room and went to meet my assessor for the afternoon session. 'We'll say no more about this Jon . . . on this occasion, but don't let it happen again!'

A Personal Master-class

The rest of the day passed without further embarrassment and I sensed my assessor starting to relax as he seemed to be happy with my paddling skills. When we arrived at the last really challenging wave of the day, however, he sent me into it, sideways from both eddies, and then called me over for a chat in the eddy. He made some suggestions about my body position and the trim of the boat and sent me into the wave again and again, each time with a slightly different tip or tweak to my style.

I noticed with a feeling of gratitude that he had moved seamlessly from assessor to mentoring mode, demonstrating as he did, best practice as an assessor. He was clearly there not only to pass or fail, but to give added value to the day, so the student comes away after the assessment, hopefully with the signed piece of paper, but also with the benefit of the assessor's wealth of experience.

Five-star white-water kayak had been a target of mine for years and it was a fantastic feeling to have achieved it. I felt a real sense of fulfilment as we took the stunning drive home from the Tryweryn along the Llangollen Valley on that bright, warm spring evening. And I felt very glad to be heading home to catch up with family and the team at FGT, after yet another challenging weekend away.

The Blind Man

Back at base, we were clearly getting better equipped, better trained and busier, but our cramped little attic offices did become oppressively oven-like in the summer months.

The solution was to arrange to have two Velux windows fitted. At least we'd be able to open a window and get some fresh air up there. However, when the sun shone directly down onto our heads in the heat of the day, it was immediately apparent to me that we'd also need to order some blinds. So I organised for a local company to come and measure up, while I was away on yet another training course, and left a note in the dairy for Mac and Jan: '11 a.m. The Blind Man.'

When Jan turned to the page on the Tuesday morning, she did not know what to make of it. Why was a blind man coming to visit, how on earth would he make it up our steep attic stairs and (worse still) back down again, safely?

She asked Mac if he remembered any discussions about working with a blind or partially sighted group, which he did not. I had left no contact number or any details, so all they could do was wait until eleven o'clock to see what this was all about.

When there was a knock on the door, the guy showed up with a rule and some colour samples as arranged.

'Hello Mrs. I'm here to measure your roof lights.'

Jan heaved a huge sigh of relief as she showed him up to our attic, and down – unaided.

The Runaway Tree

As word spread about our work, the phone began to ring more and more. Mac and Jan's decision to join FGT could not have come at a better time, as there was no way I would be able to keep up with it all on my own. In addition, Tessa was by now a full-time mother with two pre-school children at home. Thankfully we also had a growing team of volunteers willing to give time at weekends and even taking leave from work to help with midweek groups and our Total Adventure Holidays.

With my new raft of qualifications in climbing, mountain walking and white-water kayaking, we saw great opportunities to build friendships and share quality time together, while increasing everyone's experience in the outdoors, by offering a series of volunteer training weekends, none of which were ever boring.

I don't think I'll ever forget our adventures at Mill Falls on the River Usk, during one of our regular white-water kayak training weekends. We had two distinct groups of paddlers and two SIs (Senior Instructors) to lead them. Ian, a Wing Commander by day and kayak SI with FGT at weekends, was very clear that he felt his role was to lead those paddlers who were newer to the sport, while I should take the 'head bangers'. Not being much of an acrobat in a kayak myself, this would not have been my natural choice, but Ian was the volunteer so he naturally got to decide.

The section we had decided to paddle on the second day of our weekend was on the River Usk from Talybont to Llangynidir, a beautiful stretch of river with almost continuous rapids. The most challenging part for river leaders, and exciting for all paddlers, is the rapid known as Mill Falls which is graded between Class 3 and Class 4, depending on water levels.

The classic approach is to stop above the rapids and take a look. There is usually a route down the left-hand side, into some fair-sized white water as the river drops down past a natural weir to the right. A small island is conveniently located just above this section offering a great starting point for paddlers to shelter behind, and affording a good view of the proposed line before setting off.

Ian and I had planned that I would take the more advanced group down the rapid, so we were all in place and ready to collect any swimmers or debris, if any of his group capsized on their way down, and failed to roll back up. With my group safely at the bottom of the rapid, Ian was getting ready to lead his group down, one after the other, like a mother duck leading her ducklings.

As he paddled over to the island to have a look at the line for himself, we all heard an ear-splitting crack followed by a scraping, screeching sound. I was amazed to see the large tree, at the lower end of the island, shudder and then start to advance towards Ian, still upright but slanted at a crazy angle.

Ian had no choice but to get moving and try to stay out of the way of the tree, which could fall on top of him at any time. We all watched, riveted, as Ian paddled furiously out from behind the island and down the rapid. The tree started to follow, jolting as it hit rocks and dropped down the small series of small falls, but still varyingly upright.

It really looked as if the tree was chasing Ian, not catching him thank goodness, but certainly keeping pace. Ian kept paddling as fast as he could to get away from his pursuer, negotiating the rapid skilfully as he paddled towards us! As he reached the bottom of the white water and came to join us by the right hand bank, the tree lurched to the left, collapsed horizontally and was carried on down the river.

To this day there are trees caught immovably on the bridge stanchions at Llangynidir Bridge a mile downstream of Mill Falls, and whenever I take a group down this section of river, I find myself wondering if it was any of these that I had witnessed, marching from its island home in pursuit of an unsuspecting Wing Commander and his kayak.

Getting Our Bearings

During this time we were also starting to get calls to deliver training courses for other organisations and adventure clubs. It is always wonderful to have the chance to coach in the beauty and grandeur of the natural world. There is no doubt that the outdoors is a great teacher, and it is a good feeling when we find ourselves working in close cooperation with our surroundings.

One example which appeared almost too neat, almost as if I and the prevailing mountain weather systems had planned it, occurred in Snowdonia on a mountain walking skills weekend I had been asked to run for a walking club from Henley.

Everyone looked the part as we gathered after breakfast outside our base, an MoD-owned cottage in the Ogwen Valley. The group were properly equipped for a day on the hill with good-quality walking boots, waterproofs and gaiters.

Each held at the ready their map and compass in preparation for our first morning looking at mountain navigation, and I think some were a little disappointed when I suggested we put our compasses away: 'We'll need our compasses when visibility is really bad. Let's first learn to interpret what we see around us and relate it to the map. We'll come back to the compass later on.'

It was about three hours later, and after a climb of about 600 metres, that we all gathered in a sheepfold somewhere on the ridge between Glyder Fawr and Glyder Fach. I suggested we pull out our compasses and look at how we use them: 'Just imagine that a band of low cloud has come in and we need to find the right direction from here to the next peak. What bearing would we need to walk on?'

Having explained the relationship of the compass to the map, we agreed a bearing that would take us safely to our next landmark. We were just getting ready to leave the shelter of our sheepfold when we were completely surrounded by thick cloud. Visibility went down to about ten metres, the wind whistled around our heads and the temperature must have dropped several degrees. At this point we absolutely needed our compasses; a walk in the wrong direction could have led us straight over the edge of a very precipitous cliff and a drop of 200 metres.

I am not sure this can really be described as a visual aid, since lack of visibility was in fact the problem! Yet it was certainly a reality check and the perfect illustration of the importance of knowing how to use a compass, when conditions demanded.

17.

On First Inspection

Another significant, if largely unplanned part of our development at this time, came in the form of a request from one of our trustees for his son, Ben, to join our team for a few months before heading for university and a teaching career. Ben joined us to gain experience in youth work and adventure provision with our growing client list of schools and youth groups, and to help with general duties around the office and our stores, which were still in the borrowed barns of two generous local farmers.

We were also joined at this time by Rachel Allen, a member of our church, and good friend of Anita's, who'd been such a God-send around our little office before Mac and Jan had arrived. Rachel approached us to ask if we would consider involving her in our team on a voluntary basis, 3 days each week. She would work the other 2 days a week at Argos in Oxford, to earn enough to live on.

Rachel had an obvious gift for adventure youth work and it was not long before she started to see that a career in the outdoors could be the right path for her. We started talking about funding additional training for her and, with things growing at every level at FGT, we were soon able to offer her a full-time job as a trainee instructor.

In no time Rachel had qualified as a Climbing Wall Leader, Archery Leader, Basic Expedition Leader and Kayak Coach and was leading a number of our smaller bookings. She stayed with us four years and became an invaluable part of the team.

Growth is of course an expensive business and the work was at this stage very seasonal. It was therefore very hard when we had to let Rachel know that if FGT was to make it through the winter, we would have to ask her to take a break from us for a few weeks and join us again in the spring. I should not have been surprised to hear that she was almost immediately snapped up by another outdoor company and she never did come back to work with FGT.

One shared experience that is still impressed in both our memories was the day after Rachel passed her assessment as a kayak instructor. She was due to take the boats to meet a group for an introductory session, but said she was not comfortable reversing the van and trailer. My pragmatic response was that a kayak coach was little use if he or she could not handle a trailer, so the following morning, when the boats had to be returned to the barn, I gave her the keys to the van and asked her to put the boats away, which meant reversing it into a reasonably tight spot between a combine harvester and a large agricultural trailer.

My reasoning was there is no substitute for practice and she would have as long as she needed to get it right, with no one watching. She may not have been the happiest person when she drove away with the trailer in tow, but she eventually came back having spent half the morning grappling with the dark arts of trailer reversing, leaving it neatly parked.

As centre manager of a large outdoor education centre today, it has been great to see how the experience gained and the skills learned during her time with FGT have helped equip her for a career in the outdoors – and her own ministry of encouragement through adventure education.

Ben and Rachel marked the beginning of what was to become a full-time Adventure Training Gap Year. Some have said that the gap year itself has an even more profound impact on those that join the team, than our work with hundreds of children and young people every year.

One of our staff team recently described us as a 'training and sending organisation' and I suddenly realised the truth of this. Our gap-year training programme has seen nearly one hundred young adults embarking on a variety of careers including teaching, activity coaching, adventure leadership and many others. This, of course, multiplies the impact of FGT one hundredfold, as they go on equipped and inspired, into arenas of service we cannot follow.

At this time, rumours were running like wildfire through the adventure activity industry that a whole new raft of legislation and regulation was about to hit us all. Up until then, there was no compulsory regulation of the provision of activities for young people in the UK. Guidelines were published by the governing bodies for each sport, including the British Canoe Union (BCU), the Royal Yachting Association (RYA) and the Mountain Leader Training Board (MLTB), but there was no legal requirement to follow them.

The trigger for this close interest by government in the adventure activities industry was the tragic loss of four teenage lives in a kayaking accident in Lyme Bay in March

1993. A combination of inexperienced leaders, inadequate kit, low water temperatures and a strengthening off-shore breeze resulted in the boats being swamped as they were blown further out into the bay. The four teenagers had died by the time the alarm had been raised and the party was rescued. Both the activity centre and its owner were convicted of corporate manslaughter.

There was a feeling in the government that a response was needed and The Activity Centres (Young Persons' Safety) Act 1995 was passed in January 1995 and The Adventure Activities Licensing Authority (AALA) was then established under the guidance of the Health and Safety Executive. A system of inspection was published for any paid providers of adventure activities for young people, with the exception of schools, clubs and the uniformed organisations such as Scouts and Guides.

In actual fact, FGT already followed the newly published requirements of instructor qualifications, ratios and other aspects of good practice, so we did not have to change our operation as it related to adventure activity provision. But it did create a mountain of additional paperwork prior to our application for our first license. This was one mountain we would have to negotiate back at the office, from behind a desk!

While much of the additional evidence and protocols would have become necessary anyway as our operation continued to grow, these new developments created a huge workload over that winter and spring. Eventually we heard that we were due to be inspected during the week when we were running activities for a primary school in May 1997.

Our inspection was set for the Tuesday morning of a 5-day residential for a large primary school. On top of all the preparations for the week, there was now even more to do in readiness for our first HSE Inspection.

Part of the issue for us, and for so many activity providers, was fear of the unknown. On this first round of inspections, no one really knew what our inspector might want to see. One fact was very clear in our minds, however: if she didn't like what she saw, she could stop our operation there and then and ultimately could have us closed down!

Adding to the sense of challenge was the exciting news that Mac had now passed his RYA instructor ticket. We had accordingly arranged to provide sailing for the children at a local sailing club. So while Mac and the team went to prepare the sailing gear and a climbing session on our home-built wall, I met Jan, our inspector, and took her to our offices so she could check our paperwork first before heading out to see the activities, which by then should be in full swing.

I wonder what she must have thought as we arrived at the Old School House, next to our 15th-century church, and climbed the steep attic stairs into our now very crowded offices.

After reading our pristine new-look Risk Assessments and Health and Safety Plans, she asked to see how we stored records of our staff and volunteers including evidence of their qualifications. When I asked if there were any particular records she'd like to look at she selected the team which was working that week and would shortly be going out to meet. 'Let's start with the volunteer who is running climbing for you,' she said.

Our climber this week was once again Graham Harris, my good friend and outdoor mentor. In addition to his passion for the outdoors, Graham was also known for his unrelenting sense of humour and when we had asked him to send in his certificates he had really gone to town and given us far more than we had needed to ensure we had a comprehensive record of his life achievements to date.

I looked on in increasing horror as our HSE Inspector pulled out our climbing instructor's certificate for first place in a 'Bonny Baby Competition' in Roundwood Park in 1964. This was followed by Grade 1 CSE Woodwork and Grade 4 CSE German!

The inspector's eyebrows furrowed and she looked questioningly at me. I falteringly suggested that there might also be something to vouch for his skills as a climber and white-water canoeist, if she kept at it! Thankfully, Graham is as thorough and reliable as he is crazy and all we needed was to be found in his folder . . . eventually.

Along with an impressive quiver of other qualifications, our inspector was also an RYA Coach so she was immediately interested to learn that Mac had just qualified as a sailing instructor. Having seen his certificate, she asked to be escorted straight to the sailing club to see how he was getting on.

Knowing that Mac would have his hands full leading his first ever session on what was a very blustery day, I suggested that perhaps we took a detour via the climbing first, emphasising that it was a climbing wall we had built ourselves. Unfortunately and predictably, our canny inspector saw right through my attempt to pique her interest and buy Mac some more time. Whilst sounding interested in the design of the wall, she suggested we keep on course for the sailing club, and Mac's first session.

We were not to know that we were about to witness one of the most unusual and engaging spectacles I have seen during my career in the outdoors. Hearing about the situation later, I understood from Mac that he had set up all the Topper sailing dinghies on the little beach beside the sailing club, each with two primary school children on board. The arrangement with Martin, his co-leader, was that he was to send one boat out at a time, to allow the children to start to get the hang of handling their boat in the wind. Once Mac was happy each crew had grasped the concept of pushing the tiller away, as well as releasing the main sheet if they felt the boat was going too fast or might tip, Mac would signal for Martin to send out the next boat.

Sadly though, Martin had not fully grasped the plan and when Mac was out on the lake in the safety boat and ready to receive just the first boat, he gave the prearranged signal to Martin. At this point Martin sprang into action and immediately sent all five Toppers out onto the lake one after the other, in quick succession!

I could do little but stand beside our inspector and watch as a scene of general mayhem unfolded before us. Mac's morning had suddenly become frenetically busy as he buzzed between all the boats offering advice here, there and everywhere. Then, for no apparent reason, his small safety boat stopped in the water and he seemed to lose interest in his sailors.

If I was intrigued, our inspector was fascinated.

We saw Mac reach for his small oars, which are always a wise precaution in a power boat in case there is a malfunction with the engine or the fuel runs dry. In this case, the cotter pin which keeps the propeller engaged had sheared off, rendering the outboard useless. We just stood there open-mouthed, rooted to the spot, staring at Mac's frantic efforts to reach one of the boats which had inconveniently capsized right at that moment.

I don't think I have ever seen anyone row a cumbersome inflatable dinghy with such vigour, hampered by the weight of a hefty, but totally useless, outboard motor. To the best of my knowledge, he did not pull any muscles or do himself any lasting damage, and to his credit he arrived in good time to rescue two children and right the capsized dinghy.

Once again I suggested that Jan might be interested in inspecting the design of our home-designed climbing wall. Once again she declined saying she was keen to stay and watch how the session unfolded. Between them both, Mac and Martin managed to coach the kids on this moderate-sized sailing club lake, so that by the time they got off the lake they had all had a healthy taster of the sport of sailing, and a well-deserved appetite for lunch!*

A Nervous Wait

In the event, the first inspection was successful at a number of levels. There had been some concern in the outdoor education community that the HSE would send inspectors into the field armed only with a clipboard and scant understanding of

---

* Our subsequent precaution of keeping a spare cotter pin with us when running sessions with a safety boat has never been questioned.

our complex and varied industry. In fact, Jan was an excellent example of the calibre of people the AALA managed to recruit as inspectors. She was a highly qualified and widely experienced outdoor professional who knew enough to see the bigger picture and was not there to dictate how she would run the centre, but to offer quality advice.

So now it was a matter of waiting. If the inspector was happy with what she saw we stood to be granted a one-year licence to operate. If she was really confident with our infrastructure and provision, we could be given a two-year licence. As there was a cost of several hundred pounds for each inspection, the two-year licence was of course the preferred option, but this was unlikely as we were a growing organisation, offering a wide range of activities to a varied client group at a number of different activity venues across the UK. Jan would have to be thoroughly satisfied with every aspect of our provision for FGT to be awarded a two-year licence.

My main goal had been simply to get through our first inspection – not only of our activity delivery but also of our new management systems and paperwork – without any major cautions or enforced interruption in service. The letter from HSE arrived about one month later with the news that we had been granted a licence to operate . . . for two years!

18.

A Bigger Picture

The inspection was only one aspect in another busy year as word continued to spread about our adventure provision. Things seemed to be growing on every front. We were delighted when Parkgate School got in touch to say that they would be bringing three groups down to us the following year.

I had been discussing with the headteacher the relative benefits of bringing the group away at the start of Year 6, in the autumn rather than in the summer term, because it seemed a shame to gain all this fresh knowledge of their pupils at the very end of their time in the school.

The teachers we worked with often commented on the bonding that was evident during the group's time away, as well as the fresh insights they gained into each pupil, especially the apparently quiet ones. The tighter knit group could then offer so much more in leadership right through their final year, if they could benefit from their time away together before Christmas.

The headteacher must have appreciated these ideas because she called before the end of term to say that in addition to bringing her Year 6 in June, she also wanted to bring two groups to us in October.

A Growing Family at Home . . . And All Change at Work

Two other important personalities in our growing family appeared on the scene during this period of rapid growth. Emily Grace was with us all through the hot summer months of 1997, accompanying Tessa everywhere during our third year of Total Adventure Holidays. She was born shortly afterwards in late August! Lucy Dawn, our youngest child, joined the team just 16 months later in January 1999, and on the home front, at least, our period of expansion was complete.

Meanwhile at work things just kept getting busier. Summers were filling up, with more demand for our Birch Bay Ranch-style Total Adventure Holidays, and school terms were ever busier with school and youth group bookings.

With our larger team working around each other in our tiny attic offices, we all began to feel that work from these offices was fast becoming unsustainable. In the summer, the heat in those two tiny, poorly insulated rooms was intense. It began to feel to me very like our office was a seed, just before germination, jam-packed with potential and ready to burst out of its warm, restricted confines. But where were we to go to?

I was at Cokethorpe setting up what was to be our final summer there when I picked up a copy of the Witney Gazette, our local paper, and read that a Mr and Mrs Brown had decided to stop breeding cats for research in two units on their local farm, a practice which had resulted in widely reported riots across the town.

'Surely a youth education charity would be a less controversial tenant?' I thought. I contacted the Browns to ask if they might be interested in leasing the buildings to us. We arranged to meet and when I visited the property I realised how ideal the buildings would be.

There was more than ample space for our work stations and for all of our equipment and gear, and, with wipe-able waterproof flooring, there would be no problem bringing in dripping waterproofs and buoyancy aids at the end of wet activity sessions. The building was equipped with a large external door for ease of loading and unloading our minibuses and there were even two showers for our team. Mr Brown was also able to offer us on-site parking for our minibuses and trailers. This was our first opportunity to locate our offices and kit in one place, and would make the start and end of every session we ran so much more efficient.

I still held in the back of my mind, however, an image of a barn set on a hill above the River Windrush, which I had spotted on an early reconnaissance of the river by canoe, shortly after we had moved to Witney. I had seen it when we had stopped for lunch and the thought struck me that it would make a superb base for our operations.

That was now some years in the past and I had not been able to find that building since, although I had often wondered where it was. It was only when I was returning to our base from a hike along the Windrush with some local young people about three years later that I looked up and saw our minibuses parked in the barn above us, and realised with a jolt that we were in the very barn I had spotted all those years before, without even realising it!

Growing Team – Quantity and Quality

As the work developed and grew, it was becoming apparent to us all that we would need help if we wanted to keep pace with the growing opportunities we had to work alongside increasingly diverse groups of young people.

Two couples came alongside us at this time, and proved to be a huge boost as we brought our work forward into the next chapter. We had just run what was to be our last Total Adventure Holiday at Cokethorpe, and I researched another school with fantastic outdoor facilities, right on the banks of the River Avon. We decided to hold our Total Adventure Reunion there, to introduce our campers to the site, and whet their appetite for the summer.

With ever growing calls upon our services, we advertised for a 'multi-qualified, experienced outdoor pursuits professional' to join our team as a 'Senior Instructor'. We were delighted to receive a very positive response from a married couple, both of whom were qualified in a number of activities, and so we invited Ted and Helen North to join us at this Reunion, to meet the team and see if they liked us.

It was to be one of Ted's hallmarks that he brought a restless creativity with him, and in addition to slotting into our planned programme of activities, they brought the extra dimension of a squadron of stunt kites! By the end of the Reunion, it was clear to us all that both Ted and Helen would become highly valued and much-loved members of the growing team.

The other couple to come alongside our growing team during this period was Ian and Christine Brown. They had been great friends of Mac and Jan's in the Netherlands, where together they had helped run the youth work for the English-speaking church in Voorschoten. In addition to being key leaders at our Total Adventure Holidays, and helping to lead our gap-year programme, Ian brought an amazing background in business development and corporate training.

So, whilst Ian worked wonders in helping organise the many files and systems that were a necessary part of our growing company, Christine helped with the ever-increasing amounts of background admin. She even took on the daunting role of trying to get me organised . . .

19.

Total Adventure – A Lasting Difference

One of the things that had impressed us so much at Birch Bay Ranch was the huge impact it made on the campers, not just for a week but over many years, as most of the kids seemed to want to come back every summer. This left me asking a fundamental question. Would the same formula work in the UK? Summer camps are such a key part of North American culture that it was almost expected that children and teenagers spent at least a week or two of their summer at camp.

Our clear aim when we set up Total Adventure Holidays was to give the children such a great time that they would want to come back every year, and come back as leaders when they were older, just as the team had managed to do at Birch Bay. If we could achieve this, then we too would create a thread of encouragement running right through the teenage years and into young adulthood.

Recollections of the frantic experience of setting up the first Total Adventure Holidays gave way to happier memories of so many children loving the activities, and responding to the exciting content of our evening Roadshow (our version of

Birch Bay's camp fire). We began to see the same faces year after year – it was brilliant for us to see that the formula of wall-to-wall fun in a positive Christian environment was just as relevant and appealing to our British young people as it was to their Canadian cousins.

Looking back over 18 years of Total Adventure (TA) Holidays there are countless campers that became good friends as they became part of the regular TA picture, and eventually joined our team as leaders.

The two sisters, Lizzie and Louise, spring to mind, alongside Claire and Sophie. Or the two brothers Chris and James, and Matt and Sam, each of whom then joined us for a gap year.

I hope one trio, known as Team JAG, will allow me to share briefly their story across a number of years at Total Adventure, until they were old enough to join our leadership team. They then went on to develop their own ministries.

Joe was bound to be known initially as Sam's younger brother. But we soon got to know him as quite a character in his own right. He'd been coming to TA ever since he was old enough to join us, but it was some years later, when he was in his mid-teens, that I remember a slightly crazy conversation with his mother.

She had called to ask if they could hire a camping stove for him to use on a mountain expedition, as part of our Easter Adventure Holiday. I was just agreeing that we could put in a meths stove for Joe, and that of course we'd cover its safe use, when we were both stopped in mid-discussion by the loud persistent blaring of an alarm.

I asked if Mrs Travis needed to go and find out what on earth was going on, offering to call back later, but she reassured me that there was nothing to worry about. It was just Joe cooking his lunch in the kitchen. He'd set off the smoke alarm again! Ironic I thought, grinning as I put the phone down.

Andy came as a camper to TA when he was 12 and loved the activities but was not particularly there for the Roadshow or the Discussed-in-Dorm times. It happened that I was our speaker at Total Adventure that year and he came up to me one evening at the end of the Roadshow and asked if he could have a Bible. I gave him mine and I wrote in the cover for this 12-year-old lad: 'Keep this until you come back as a leader – Eph 2:10.'

Greg, like Andy, was there for the sport and definitely not for the 'God stuff'. But he loved the activities at TA and the sense of fun and belonging he found in the dorm groups. He also really appreciated the Dorm Leaders, who managed to mix the serious business of having fun, with the fun business of getting to know more about God.

As Joe, Andy and Greg returned to TA over successive summers, they found themselves in the same dorm each year and became fast friends. Eventually the time came for them to be leaders and all three signed up for our gap year.

In the course of that year, living in the same staff house, they became known as Team JAG and remain good friends. They have each now gone on into very different walks of life, and opportunities to share the hope they have grasped with others:

Joe is now helping run a centre called Teen Ranch in south-east Scotland. He has even used those skills helping set up Christian adventure camps in Poland and Kenya. Greg went on to qualify and work as a primary school teacher in south London, and, together with his wife Sophie, has just returned from their first year setting up One Way Pre-School in Zimbabwe, in cooperation with the local church in Harare.

Andy met me recently for a catch up in London, where he is now in business selling high-quality suits to business-men in the City. Obviously he needs to dress appropriately and has his own bespoke suits made for when he is in sales mode. He recently told me that the verse I'd written in that Bible all those years ago has been his favourite Bible verse ever since – Ephesians 2:10 had been one of the verses I'd referred to at the Roadshow that evening. It talks about how we are God's workmanship, created unique and different, 'to do good works, which God prepared in advance for us to do'.

What I didn't know was that Andy has the words 'God's Masterpiece' embroidered into the chest pocket of each suit that is made for him, as a reminder of how special he is in God's eyes and the real reason we have each been given our unique mix of skills and talents – to use them in his service.

When I wrote to ask if he'd mind me sharing this story, he replied, 'Of course. The exact words you wrote in my Bible were: "Keep this until you come back as a leader – Eph 2:10." I kept that book until I was a leader, then I passed it on to one of my dorm who didn't have a Bible. I kept it until I was a leader – just as instructed!'

What an encouragement to realise that even such a small thing as a sentence and a verse written in a pocket Bible, can stay with someone right through their teens and on into their adult life. What a privilege to be part of such a life changing work!

It is a wonderful thing that guys like Joe, Andy and Greg, and several hundred besides, are inspired by our input into their lives over just a few short weeks of summer camp. And we in turn are so much more encouraged when we hear about it years later.

The Total Adventure Song

Perhaps the spirit of Total Adventure is best caught in the words of the TA song, which was written for our TA Holidays some years earlier:

You are Lord of All and I've been told that you love me.
Sun, moon and stars were made at your command.
And yet you love me and there's nothing on earth
Can shake me out of your hand.

You gave me friends who've helped me see you more clearly,
Through them I've seen your love and had such fun,
They've shown me how to keep my feet on the ground
And point the way to the Son.

> May my walk talk,
> May my talk talk,
> But may my walk talk louder than my talk talks

Now I know I can live the Total Adventure
With you the Lord of All at my right hand.
I know you'll help me keep my feet on the rock,
And stay well clear of the sand.

Come join the party, live the Total Adventure,
The Lord of heaven and earth will guide you through.
He knows your weaknesses but he'll give you strength,
Here's what he's asking of you:

Let your walk talk,
Let your talk talk,
But let your walk talk louder than your talk talks

You are Lord of All and yet you'll love me for ever,
Though I may never know how much you care.
Wherever I may be, whatever I face,
I know you'll always be there.

If young people, from whatever background leave the Adven-ture*Base* with the assurance that they are greatly loved and never alone, and that they can always come back to share their achievements and challenges, to a place where there will always be a welcome, *that* is a life-changer. Who knows what they will go on to do with that reassurance and knowledge in their own lives as their story unfolds. This is the heart of what our work at Adventure*Plus* and the Adventure*Base* is all about.

20.

River of Life

In addition to our Instructor Training Gap Year, we also run a number of other training courses each year for our volunteers and others.

Although these are open courses – we may get instructors from other commercial centres, freelance coaches or Army Physical Training Instructors – we always start our day with a morning thought in addition to the day's briefing. Even these short morning thoughts can make a surprising impact on the participants that we may not be aware of at the time.

I remember one white-water kayak coach training course we ran on some of our beautiful rivers in south-west England. We had a number of external trainees, in addition to a couple of our own team, and I was due to lead the morning briefing on the Sunday, and therefore the morning thought too.

I decided to borrow from what is probably my favourite section of the Gap-Year programme: 'Out there – in him'. I have always liked this phrase, which was first coined by John-Luke, a former Gap-Year Coordinator. It captures two linked but different themes: that there is so much we can learn about our Creator, from his creation, and also that when we are out in the beauty of it all, both in the fun times and when life gets hard, we are of course always in God's hand (John 10:29).

That morning I decided to share some thoughts about the amazingly consistent and abundant flow that is a river. As white-water kayakers we could relate to this, but it is very easy to take something reliable like a river for granted. However, if we stop and think about it for a moment, it is amazing to realise that a wave on a river is not a static object. It is an unceasingly recreated, moving dynamic flow of water that has to be constantly renewed.

We had picked the River Barle for this second day of the course, as it combines a beautiful river journey with a good variety of moving water features on which to practice our eddy turns, breaking in and out and 'ferry glides' across the flow. But these manoeuvres were only made possible because we knew we could count on the ongoing renewed supply of moving water.

In our morning thought I picked up the concept that the waves we were going to find that day had been forming and reforming all through the night, whilst we'd been asleep . . . In fact they had been there, no doubt, on the day I was born; or when Henry VIII was crowned King of England; or when William the Conqueror or Julius Caesar had first invaded our shores.

What an amazing abundance of constant flow, not just when we wanted to get on and play in the waves, but all day and night, every day and night, for centuries gone and doubtless for centuries to come. I closed the meeting with a brief reading from Revelation about the river of life. We recognised that the river we would be paddling on that day offered us a fantastic reminder of the extravagant flow of life in the world around us, and of the river of God's love, which like this physical river, would flow on unceasing.

As paddlers we knew the fun we had in store and we were eager to get going. We had an amazing day playing on the standing waves and in the stoppers, up and over haystacks and in and out of eddies; and I trust the guys on the course took away some helpful tips on kayaking in such a lively environment.

It was not until some hours later, on the way home in the minibus, that the topic of our morning thought came up again in conversation. I was driving and Tim was the only other guy left awake as we rumbled north up the M5 towards Oxfordshire. I knew he'd once had a strong faith but had moved away from his walk with God whilst he was away at Uni.

We'd been sitting in silence for a while. I'd been concentrating on driving the van and kayak trailer into the night when Tim spoke over the hum of the engine.

'Thanks Jon for what you shared this morning . . . You know, I might come back to God, some day'.

The classic Christian response would be one of immediate joy at this exciting news, but there was another side to my reply which somehow rang true for this conversation.

'That's great Tim,' I replied, 'but whilst that would be great news for you, and for you that changes everything, on the much bigger scale, in another way, it doesn't change anything.'

I sensed his surprise and I knew I had his attention.

'You see the River of God will flow on regardless, like that river today. We knew the fun that was to be had and the river was there for us to enjoy, but we had the choice: to get on it and paddle and train and play, or to walk away. What a shame that would have been had we walked away – what a great day we would have missed!

'But you know the river isn't going to stop flowing just because you or I choose not to get on it and paddle – or dive in and swim. That river, like God's love, is going to flow on regardless and nothing I do will ever change that – thank goodness. It's up to us if we choose to throw ourselves on it . . . or just walk away.'

We left it like that and the conversation moved on. What might sound a little harsh when read in black and white just seemed the right response at the time. I am delighted to report that Tim is now very active in the youth ministry of his local church, and we remain good friends!

There is so much that we can learn about our Creator God from his amazing and beautiful creation. It is an amazing classroom and training environment for adults and young people alike and the truth remains, when we are out there, we are always 'out there – in him'.

That was some years ago, but I will be planning a couple of other River Leader courses in the coming year, and I am already looking forward to another fun day on that stunning Somerset river as it rushes down from ancient Tarr Steps towards the edge of Exmoor and on, into the River Exe and the sea.

I imagine it will still be there!

21.

A Capital Conundrum

Although by now we were working with a regular stream of different youth organisations, and our Total Adventure Holidays were growing in popularity every year, we had still not found a permanent site for an adventure centre. Every group we worked with would meet us at the river or the crag, or we'd book them into a residential centre.

So what were we missing? I found myself wrestling with this question over a number of years. Indeed, I had not stopped looking for potential sites since the outcome of the Public Enquiry had resulted in the one property we had been offered becoming the subject of a compulsory purchase order. But nothing had looked or felt right, or been affordable. Unlike so many other charity-owned outdoor centres, we did not have the backing of a wealthy supporter or landowners who wanted their property to be used for such valuable work.

I regularly reported to our Trustees on this issue and we soon identified a run of events that we came to know as 'the Capital Conundrum'. Every time we heard that a suitable property had come on the market and we started to get even remotely interested, we would then have to engage the support of potential backers. Any serious supporters would only take a property proposal seriously if we had managed to organise some sort of deal with the owners, and had secured appropriate planning permission, all of which takes considerable time and expense. By the time we had this organised, another buyer would come along and the property would be sold.

How then could we continue to develop our work with growing numbers of young people, which in itself brought ever-increasing costs, and somehow entertain the idea of securing a property, which in our part of the UK would have a substantial price tag?

One day the answer hit me with surprising and unexpected clarity. And the answer was obvious: 'Just get on and do the job you are here to do. The original aim of all this was to challenge and encourage young people to "live the adventure of faith", not necessarily to build a centre.'

Nothing had changed. That was to remain the focus of our work. And seemingly against all the odds, we were being very successful doing just that.

It's About People, Not Property

Our Christian heritage encourages us to look at the life of Jesus as a model for our actions, and when I thought about some of the key points in his life, I suddenly realised that even for him, the King of Kings and Lord of Lords, property was not an issue.

He was born in a manger or feeding trough, in the borrowed stable of a publican; the last supper took place in an upper room, lent to him for the occasion; on Palm Sunday, he rode into Jerusalem on a borrowed donkey; his crown of thorns, his purple gown and the cross, were all provided for the purpose; even his tomb belonged to a man named Joseph.

The message to me at the time was clear. Don't become fixated on getting a property; keep your focus on what you are called to do – to encourage people to 'live the adventure of faith'; or as I had heard our friends at Abernethy say, 'Keep the main thing, the main thing!'

It is hard to capture the sense of release and relief, when we finally grasped the reality of following his lead and laying aside our own ambition. It removed the burden of trying to force an issue that was not right for that time. It also freed us to focus fully on the job in hand and it gave us a clear answer when so many people were asking about progress in our work to set up a centre.

Reorganising and Rebranding

One result of the growth of the organisation was the sense that it was right to convert our original charitable trust to a company with charity status, bringing the big advantage to our Trustees of transferring their status to that of directors of a limited company. Up until that time they were, as trustees, liable for the actions of our growing team!

As part of that process, we felt it was also right to review the name, Fair Glade Trust, looking for something that would capture more of our now thriving work as a busy adventure provider. The importance of this came home to me more forcefully when I received a letter at the Fair Glade Trust offices asking if we would be interested in developing our range of air fresheners!

After some weeks of deliberation and prayer, it was Nigel, our long-term volunteer sailing instructor and Fiat Panda

4x4 tow truck operator, who reminded us of a name we had first coined years ago when setting up those original sports holidays with Christians in Sport.

We had suggested Sports*Plus* should be the name of the sports side of the holidays and left Adventure*Plus* as a possible idea for some point in the future for our own brand of adventure youth work, if we ever felt the need to change the name from Fair Glade Trust. I was in no doubt that now was the right time to make the change.

Everyone felt the name Adventure*Plus* captured our main focus, to encourage people to 'live the adventure' of their lives, whilst the 'Plus' brought in the bigger perspective of our Christian heritage. A web search revealed that the name was not already in use, and the web addresses were also still available.

We registered the name with Companies House, as a Company Limited by Guarantee, and Adventure*Plus* was born. This was quickly shortened to A+, the mark every school group wants to achieve, and of course it is our hope that any course we run leaves people with 'A-positive' experience!

Vision and Mission

As the coming months were to reveal, this was clearly the season of new beginnings. By now we had been joined by a number of other staff and the gap-year programme had developed into a professional instructor training year.

Managing a growing organisation requires a very different skill set from the solo entrepreneurial role of getting a new project off the ground. It was time to put some structure into the general business. A series of meetings was set up to discuss the right way forward, focusing on what work we considered central to the core mission of the organisation and what, if any, we should leave behind.

A mission statement and set of core principles were agreed, by which we measured everything we were asked to do. We identified four key sections of A+:

MAP: **M**obile **A**dventure*Plus*, would handle any group bookings, the largest sector of our work, delivering adventure provision for schools, youth groups, churches and other organisations.

Total Adventure Holidays™: for individuals, similar in ethos and programme to our experiences of Birch Bay Ranch. The long-term positive influence on the lives of so many young people there had been the original inspiration at the start of FGT.

DisTIL™: Our reshaped gap-year programme, incorporating the elements captured in the name: **Dis**cipleship, **T**raining **I**nstructor and **L**eadership.

Adventure*Impact*™: At this point, we also saw the need to develop a specialist unit to work with young people struggling with the pressures of teen life in their everyday environment: those at risk of exclusion from school or who might already have a criminal record. We knew we had neither the funds nor the manpower, but the seed was sown and we planned to make it happen at some point, hopefully in the not too distant future. The unit is now known to many who participate in these programmes as Adventure*Impact*™.

22.

Serious Fun

It all started with a single phone call.

'Hi, my name's Andy. I work for The Nehemiah Project in south London with men who want to leave behind their lives of violence and addiction. Many have been in prison but are now living in our care and working hard to sort themselves out. Every year we organise a holiday for them and I was wondering if you could provide accommodation and a series of adventure days for us in the Forest of Dean.'

The potential of adventure activities for building trust and teamwork between Andy's team and the guys in their care was clear and exciting. I launched straight into the benefits of tandem open canoes, where each pair has to work together, and he seemed to like what he was hearing.

When I continued to describe the trust element of climbing, describing how the guys could manage each other's safety rope, and *his*, I sensed a certain caution at the other end of the phone. Andy knew the history of some of the guys on the programme and he was clearly not very reassured by the thought of trusting his life to some of them as he dangled from the rocky crags of Symonds Yat.

We eventually settled on a date and a programme and I arrived with a van full of gear and a trailer of canoes, just ahead of the group.

After dinner, the first item on the programme was a night hike, which took us to a disused railway tunnel about two miles away, which is half a kilometre long! As we all set off into the twilight, I was aware that the general banter, whilst good natured, had a sharper edge to it than I was used to. The guys immediately latched onto anything that could be unpicked or misconstrued, so everyone had to be on their guard to some extent. Their leadership team informed me that this was not unusual and was a product of their experience of life 'inside'.

The guys all seemed pretty macho and up for an adventure but I was slightly concerned that the activities we had planned might not challenge them enough. I was therefore surprised by the reaction of some in the group when we entered the tunnel.

By now, night had descended and the gloom seemed to thicken around us as we entered the mouth of the tunnel. As we trudged deeper towards the middle of this 500m-long artificial cave, the darkness became profound. There seemed to be absolutely no light at all, and I sensed a real nervousness amongst some of the group who were clearly disturbed by this deep blackness. Many were holding each other's shoulders or backpacks for support as we eventually emerged at the other end, to be immediately amazed by the detail we could make out in the apparent darkness of the evening. The silhouette of trees against the night sky and the outline of the hill above the tunnel were all remarkably clear; we could even make out the shadowy figures of the rest of the group moving around us, deep in the railway cutting.

When I suggested going back through the tunnel one by one and in silence, there were some for whom this was almost too much. It would be inappropriate to write here the details of the debrief we shared when we emerged from the tunnel again, but suffice it to say I learned a lot about the deep-seated uncertainty and fear that is often hidden beneath a macho or aggressive exterior.

As I discovered more of their history, I began to realise how much progress some of these guys had made in their struggle to leave their former lives of crime, and in some cases violence, behind. Knowing this, I would never have agreed to go to that tunnel alone with them before they had joined the programme!

Breaking In and Breaking Out!

The next morning saw us canoeing just downstream of Ross-on-Wye, and ending at the rapids of Symonds Yat. Our task was to train them in the skills they would need as we paddled down the rapid. The guys had already decided who they were going to team up with for the day and I did not want to disturb the delicate dynamics within the group. When I asked for the first pair to step forward to help demonstrate how to get into the canoe – without falling into the river – I knew we had an interesting day ahead of us as Jeff (not his real name) and Steve (nor his) stepped forward.

I don't think I have ever worked with a more solidly built individual than Jeff. He was huge, widthways and in depth, and not short either! His bull-like neck was about the same diameter as my chest and each upper arm made my thigh look feeble. When Jeff got into the back of our 17-foot long open canoe, he nearly sank the stern of the boat and it promptly assumed the angle of a speed boat about to go 'up on the plane'.

He steadied himself in his sharply inclined boat as the shorter, more slender figure of Steve stepped forward, grinning. There was nothing of him in comparison. When he got into the front of the boat the angle of incline hardly changed at all!

The pair was set to spend the rest of the day paddling around looking like a speedboat in slow motion, or a canoe with a large anchor attached to the rear end! Looking at the boat I was not sure if I should let it stay as it was or suggest a change of partners, but I was not convinced that anyone would have provided enough of a counterweight to Jeff to make very much difference anyway.

This was probably the only time I have ever taken a group out wondering, honestly, if I could actually get one of the canoeists back into his boat if he capsized. However good my rescue technique might be, if it came to my weight against Jeff's, ultimately raw physics must overrule.

A bit of background for the uninitiated: kayakers use the term 'breaking in' (to the flow) and 'breaking out' again into the flat water of an eddy. There is often a sharp transition between the fast water of a rapid and the still water behind an obstacle such as a rock or tree, which is known as the 'eddy line'. It can be very easy to capsize the boat as you cross this eddy line unless you switch your weight, and edge your boat the right way.

Long before we got to the rapid, I gathered the group by the edge of the river to talk about some of the skills we'd need at Symonds Yat. I assumed coach-mode and tried to sound appropriately focused as I walked straight into the next lot of banter:

'Okay guys, listen up!' I had everyone's attention.

'I'm going to give you some tips about breaking in.' The group all looked at me, incredulous . . . grins and winks spreading from one face to another, like a rash! 'And then we're going to learn how to break out,' I continued.

They could hold it in no longer. One or two started to snigger and then everyone burst out laughing. With my canoe coach's head on, I just did not see the joke until one of them chipped in with, 'I think we could teach you a bit about breaking in Jon! What d'ya want? A new telly or a computer? We'll sort it for ya. Don't you worry!'

'Yeah, but we're always open to tips on how to break out!'

The banter continued and we had loads of fun on the river that day. We must have learned something because my goal of having a group that looked like they knew what they were doing when they went down the rapid was achieved!

Only one boat capsized that day . . . three times! Jeff and Steve must have been successfully rescued – at least twice!

Trust Me

Climbing was next on the agenda and I went up ahead of the group to set up. I have to confess I was thinking of my new friend Jeff as I placed at least one extra anchor point for each rope. This was the experience that Andy had been nervous about over the phone, but we had got to know the group reasonably well during their stay so far and decided to continue with the plan of allowing the guys to manage the safety ropes.

There was a palpable sense of anticipation when the first guy climbed, knowing as they did the background of the guy on the other end of the rope, and therefore responsible for their safety in the event of a fall.

After a while, everyone had climbed the three routes we had set for them, so I demonstrated how a climber leads up a route from the bottom, placing protection in the cracks in the rock as he goes, as opposed to walking round to the top and dropping the rope down to the group.

It was Andy who volunteered to climb the new route first, once the safety ropes had been secured. I was still at the top looking down at him as he set off from the ground to climb up to join me, and it was one of the guys on the programme who was belaying him, closely supervised, of course, by one of our team.

What a great demonstration of new confidence within the group, between the workers and those under their care, and proof that common experiences of this kind, where real adventures are shared, really does help build relationship and trust. I call it 'The serious business of *having fun*!'

Cops and Robbers

The final day was programmed for team challenges and group initiative tests. At lunchtime, after an entertaining and enjoyable morning, one of the carers on the team shared that the group would never have managed to tackle these tasks, which required a range of communication skills including listening and supporting others, had we tried this on the first day.

Mac and I left the group at the centre, at the end of Day 3 as planned, and returned to our Oxfordshire base, knowing we had learned a lot about a sector of our community of which we had little experience, and convinced of the value of programmes like this.

We were delighted when Andy wrote to us the following week to thank us for such a successful week and to book the group in for the following year. Same time, same place. This continued for a couple of years, and after about three visits Andy got in touch to ask if we could cope with a larger group. This event, too, yielded some memorable learning experiences for everyone.

On this occasion, our team included Mark, one of our gap-year instructors who came to help me on the river, and Rich, another A+ leader, who would run the climbing, supported by my good friend Graham. Graham would be joining us after a full day's work in London so would be arriving late on that first evening.

Graham has a very varied employment history, having worked as a primary school teacher, a quantity surveyor and a policeman. In fact during his time in the Met, he had even been our local bobby in Hampstead when I'd lived in that crazy *Neighbours* house on Parliament Hill.

When he walked in to the lounge at the centre, most of the guys were gathered round a table tennis table watching me getting beaten, despite my best efforts. It was 'winner stays on', so the next game started straight away and it too was of a pretty good standard.

Then followed one of those moments when it all suddenly went quiet in the room, just as Graham whispered in my ear, 'Why are these guys all so good at table tennis?'

The silence continued but I was immediately aware of shifty glances darting around the room from face to grinning face. Then Steve, one of the guys I'd recognised from last year piped up with a broad East London smile: 'Well . . . there wasn't much else to do . . . where we've been . . .'

'Oh?' Graham shrugged.

Ten seconds later he turned to me again, the room still silent and watching him. 'Why not?'

'Come on Graham!' I thought. 'You used to be a copper . . . Wake up!'

Steve again: 'Let's just say . . . , we was inside a lot'

'Oh?' said Graham, whose mind was still clearly somewhere back near Gloucester on the A40.

Then, as his gaze went from one face to another round the room, he let out a long, revealing, 'Ooooohhhh!'

Everyone responded to Graham's slow wake-up call with wide grins, nodding heads and a long 'Yeeeeeessssssss', as they watched the penny drop – far too slowly!

Chewbacca

In general, the atmosphere amongst the group was superb and a real testament to the quality of the programme the guys had signed up to. I could not resist having a quiet word with one of the staff members towards the end of that first evening however, after a conversation with Jack, the newest guy on the programme, who had only been out of prison for about 2 weeks.

It was his father's birthday and he wanted to use the centre's payphone to call home, to wish his dad a Happy Birthday. But the rules of the programme were clear: no outside contact for the first 6 weeks. Jack was finding this really hard on this day of all days and he badly wanted to make that birthday phone call to his dad.

I said I'd have a word with one of the team. John, the leader that year, was very understanding with me as he pointed out that the rules are there for a reason. How did I know it was his dad's birthday? The chances are Jack wanted to get in touch with one of his former contacts and arrange to get some 'stuff' dropped off in the bins at the back of the centre sometime during the night. An addict will try everything to get back to the cause of his addiction when he gets the chance. This was exactly why he had signed up to be supported, in such a stringent, protective programme, when he came out of prison.

The reasoning was obvious and I kicked myself for being so easily taken in. I decided to let these guys do their job in the same way I would expect them to let me do mine, out on the river, or at the rock face.

There was only one occasion in the whole week when I caught a glimpse of how volatile these guys would have been if it had not been for the benefits of the programme they were now a part of.

We had just finished one of our team challenges, which involved filling a vertical ten-foot high pipe with water, to retrieve a message from an empty bottle, which could only be accessed by floating it up the pipe.

The rules of the game made it almost certain that most of the team would get wet trying to plug the many holes in the pipe in order to fill it to the top. Waterproofs were therefore issued and anything that might get damaged if it got wet was placed on a wall, a safe distance away.

At the end of the game, with the message successfully retrieved, there was plenty of laughter and good humour as the guys were changing out of their waterproofs and gathering up their possessions. Suddenly, out of nowhere, the atmosphere changed and I witnessed an instant flare-up of raw aggression that took me totally by surprise. Ryan, one of the bigger guys, grabbed one of the others by the scruff of the neck and put his fist up to thump him:

'Where's my snout?' he shouted. 'You've taken my snout?'

'No mate, of course I haven't got your snout!' came the immediate reply. I was reluctant to intervene, but I had to ask what was going on.

'He's nicked my t'bacca!' Ryan yelled, over his shoulder, maintaining a firm grip on the collar of the accused. 'I put a full bag of Golden Virginia on the wall with everything else and it ain't there now. He's nicked it!'

The accused was about to start to defend himself when his voice was drowned out by the surprisingly loud bleating of the centre's new billy goat which had been standing in his enclosure watching the whole 'Leaky Pipe' exercise – right beside the wall.

We all looked round to see the animal grinning insanely swaying from side to side, wide eyed, chewing a whole mouthful of Golden Virginia – plastic wallet and all! The aggression dissolved as quickly as it had flared up, lost in a peal of raucous laughter from everyone except Ryan, who faced the prospect of having to go without, until he received next month's allowance.

A Real Buzz and No Chemicals

We planned to work in two groups on the final 2 days of the holiday. I was to take half the guys canoeing, and was already bracing myself for the banter when it came to breaking in and breaking out, while Rich and Graham would take the others rock climbing.

Two separate challenges arose, one with each of the activity groups. While there was nothing particularly difficult about our river day, I was supported by a very enthusiastic, but cheeky gap-year instructor called Mark, who happened to be a very good canoeist. Known as 'Manimal' or 'Oranga-man' by our other instructors because of his impressive feats of agility and strength, this was his first time working with this kind of client group and from the outset I was concerned that he would not treat them with the respect, or caution, required.

When we got on the river he lost no time in displaying his skills with the bucket stroke. This is about the most effective way to get anyone soaked to the skin, short of throwing them in the river, and it involves shovelling up copious amounts of water with the paddle and drenching anyone who happens to be in the way. Mark took particular delight in soaking each of the guys in turn and then paddling away, impressively fast, so as not to get caught.

One character in particular that I had got to know on previous visits was not amused. I knew he had a seriously violent background and was making fantastic progress controlling his temper but Mark was not helping. He was very fit with an impressive physique. He was also an expert in a variety of martial arts, but did not have the skills of an experienced paddler. I watched time and again the muscles on his back rippling as he was determined to get back at the 'Orangaman', but whenever he put extra power into the stroke, the boat just flew off course – fast but in the wrong direction.

Mark did not help by sitting quietly in his canoe, a safe distance away, fixing his frustrated quarry with his broad Cheshire Cat grin! I honestly thought at one stage that he was going to get nailed later if he carried on, so I had a quiet word. I like to think I didn't actually save Mark's life that day, but I honestly cannot be certain.

Meanwhile, the climbers had an issue of their own. Graham and Rich were both talented climbers and leaders in the outdoors, but unfortunately for them I had made the mistake of taking an earlier group from Nehemiah up the Longstone, a tall pinnacle of rock that stands out from the rest of the cliff. Climbers feel particularly exposed as they scale this free-standing pillar, but those who make it to the top are treated to a fantastic view of the whole forest valley winding away in both directions, and of the rapids far below.

Apparently stories of this 'epic climb' had grown out of all proportion during the year and all they had talked about on their way out of London was how they too wanted to have a crack at the pinnacle.

For this particular group that would not have been appropriate, but the guys knew what they wanted and would not be put off. I was concerned about how Rich and Graham would handle the situation, knowing how hard it would be to sell anything else to these guys. Tales of the pinnacle had got the testosterone flowing, and nothing else would do. I had my hands full on the river, however, with my group and 'Manimal', so I just had to leave our climbing team to sort their own issues out.

When both groups met up in the car park at the end of the day, the climbers were absolutely buzzing. Somehow Rich and Graham had surpassed even this group's expectations and they had clearly loved it. They could not speak highly enough of their climbing instructors. Great job guys!

In fact, this had been our last day with them so we were packing gear away and preparing to go our separate ways. Before we parted, someone suggested we pray together. As we stood in a rough circle beside the A+ van, in the Forestry Commission car park, no one would have guessed the collective history of this group of guys – certainly not from the broad smiles on their faces, warmed by the late afternoon sun.

And as we prayed, I stood for a while with my eyes open, looking up at the tops of the tall conifers against the clear blue sky, appreciating the scent of the Douglas Fir and Norway Spruce blown gently on the breeze. My mind wandered back to a morning in the Rocky Mountains, more than ten years before, and that first experience of real rock climbing with a group from Birch Bay Ranch. I knew we had made the right decision to pursue this adventure of our own.

The prayer of the youngest of the guys on the programme, an ex-addict recently released from prison, and fresh out of Rich and Graham's climbing session, only served to confirm this for me, as his voice drifted into my memories:

'Dear God, I never knew you could get such a buzz. And no chemicals involved. Thank you!'

23.

Aim

Working with the team from the Nehemiah Project was never going to become dull or routine. It was a privilege to get to know these guys, as they shared some of the stories behind the struggles they had endured and some of the issues that would be with them for the rest of their lives. Particularly encouraging for me were the men who had started as residents on the programme and who were now here as part of the team, to mentor the guys who still had such huge personal battles ahead of them.

I had always felt, right from the start of our work with A+, however, that prevention is better than cure. If we could get to these men earlier in the process, before their habits led them into serious criminal activity, so much heartache would be saved. And each story of addiction and crime, of course, also hugely impacts the lives of the families of those concerned, and those who care about them. Then there is the serious impact on the lives of every victim of theft, drug pushing or the more violent crimes so often associated with addictive lifestyles.

I had wanted to set up a specialist unit working with young people at risk of exclusion from school, or those already descending into a life of crime and conviction, for some years, but growth is an expensive business, and we simply did not have the funds. I was immediately interested then, when Andy, our original contact with the Nehemiah Project, called out of the blue one January evening, just as I was preparing to leave for my five-star canoe leader assessment. Even though my head was buzzing with all the kit I needed to be sure I did not forget, this was too engaging a conversation to leave unexplored.

Adventure*Impact*

Andy wanted to know if we had considered working in a more focused way with young people caught up in this kind of chaotic lifestyle known in the trade as NEET (Not in Education, Employment or Training). I explained that this was something I had wanted to do from the outset, but that setting up a specialist unit like this would take another raft of funds that we simply did not have.

Andy's motivation was similar to my own and he had seen at first hand the trail of destruction left in the wake of the guys he had been working with. If only someone could have got to them before all that chaos. Something excited and encouraged me about the way the conversation was going. If this was important work to be doing, then money, or the lack of it, should not be allowed to prevent it. We already had so many of the required ingredients for this kind of work in place, with the activity kit, qualifications and knowledge of adventure venues around the UK.

I had obviously developed some experience of raising support for A+ over the years, and Andy had been working as a fund-raiser in recent years for the Nehemiah Project. We decided to push the door and see if there might be a future in this new initiative. Neither of us was in any doubt about the need.

Our combined professional experience, Andy with several years of hands-on work in drug rehabilitation, especially with ex-offenders, and my background in the caring professions, adventure provision and youth work, would surely strengthen any applications for financial support. So, with the approval of the A+ Board, Andy and I prepared a funding bid for a three year programme, to get Adventure*Impact* (A*im*) off the ground.

Over the following weeks we watched the post every day for letters of support that would signal the start of Adventure-*Impact*, and also a move for Andy and his family, from their home in West London, to join the A+ team in Witney.

When the first offers of support for A*im* came in, we could see that yet another dream might actually become a reality. The need for such work in our part of the country was clearly recognised and it was not long before Andy and I were discussing start dates and the logistics of moving up to Witney, with his wife Heather and young children, Cameron and Kathryn.

This marked the start of an opportunity to work with some of the young people in our community who needed to hear our message of encouragement most. So A*im*, our specialist unit was born, and A+ was now equipped to focus our expertise in yet another new direction.

Inspiring the Next Generation

As we take students who struggle to focus in the confines of a classroom into the natural world, usually for 1 day a week, over a period of 2 or 3 months, we hear amazing feedback from the schools or exclusion units that referred them to us. Encouraging reports of improved behaviour during the rest of the week, better records of attendance and increased attention span often combine to help the student make great strides too in their academic attainment.

When we hear good news of the benefits of our work to some of our most chaotic young people, such as those referred to us by the Crime Prevention Units of local Young Offender Teams, I am often reminded of Simon, that young lad from a similarly troubled background, on his last evening at Birch Bay Ranch, 20 years earlier.

He, too, saw a clear contrast with the harsh real world of his life in care. The hope he grasped when he realised the truth that he was in fact much loved and that he had a positive contribution to make was clear for all to see. That summer he resolved to put this new hope into practice in his life. I have not seen or heard from Simon for over twenty years but I have often wondered how he is doing and I still find myself praying that he continues to live in the real, brighter world he glimpsed that summer.

Perhaps that is part of the reason why I was so excited that our *Aim* team recently set up a young leader's programme, offering longer-term opportunities to any that take naturally to our approach to adventure, to train in the skills they will need if they are to develop as leaders in the outdoors.

And when I see some of these guys coming back to join our Instructor Training gap year, or volunteering alongside our A+ team, I know our original vision for Adventure*Impact* rings true, as we work to 'inspire the next generation'.

24.

The Final Chapter?

So we've arrived at the last chapter of the story, or is it in fact just the beginning of a new adventure?

Last year, A+ grew 20 per cent, working with over 6,000 children and young people. And yet, A+ does not have an adventure centre – Adventure*Base* – to which we can welcome groups with activities all set up. Every activity session begins with our team loading the kit into vans and trailers at our HQ-depot, and driving to meet the group at their venue. We then have to set up whatever activities the group has requested, be it an archery range, team-building challenges or climbing at a crag.

At the end of each session we pack down the kit, return to base and unload it into the stores, only for it to be rolled out again the next day, in a different permutation for another group in some other part of the country.

This is clearly a massive workload and it is a huge achievement of the amazing A+ team that they managed to sustain this level of activity for so many children last year, and all with such enthusiasm, commitment and a real sense of seemingly unquashable fun! There is no question that it is high time we embraced the challenge of establishing a purpose-built adventure centre. This would not only increase the number of groups and individual children we could reach, it would also improve the quality of the adventures we can offer.

So, once again, I sense the strange mix of eager anticipation and jubilant excitement anchored by the daunting prospect of a huge task ahead. The chemistry feels very similar now to when we first tried to set up a youth-work charity with a clear calling, but no experience, 20 years ago.

I have been keeping my eyes and ears open for some months now, for the right location, ideally within 20 minutes of our current offices and our very special Windrush location. That is why I found myself on the phone, early last year, with the owners of a small Christian conference centre about 20 minutes from Witney. Some years ago, they had told Tessa and me that they had heard God saying to them that 'He would use the farm to supply the needs of the saints.' Since then they had gradually developed some of their farm buildings into Windmill Farm Conference Centre, a place of encouragement and retreat.

In fact Tessa and I had been on hand to help them during this process, with some of the background practicalities of building a staff team and gearing up the accounts to handle their growing operation. We had been delighted when they took our suggestion to use part of one of the converted barns as a sports hall complete with a climbing wall and incorporated a boot room and drying room into the design of the residential unit.

Ever since it opened, A+ has been providing activities for groups who come to stay at Windmill Farm, so we know the site well. I had often thought that the land behind the conference centre might be an excellent venue for developing further activities.

Now that we were seriously thinking of developing an Adventure*Base*, I realised that the disused barn and silage clamp on the extensive land behind the conference centre would provide an ideal footprint for the buildings we would need. There was plenty of space here for the various activities we would be offering.

The land was also remote enough from the conference centre and neighbouring village to give a real sense of rural wilderness, yet still be accessible for groups staying at the conference centre to use the adventure training facilities we'd be creating on site. It couldn't be better if we'd planned it ourselves!

It was therefore with some trepidation that I picked up the phone to call Richard and Rosemary, the owners, to ask if they might consider selling some of the land at the back of their centre to A+. I sensed a certain distance when I outlined the plan, and not just because they were in Shetland at the time. Yet they agreed to consider what I had suggested and said they would come back to me soon. I was therefore intrigued when they called a couple of days later and suggested we meet up when they were next in the area.

'We were a little taken aback,' Rosemary began, 'by your phone call, not least the timing of it. What you were not to know was that just a day or two beforehand we'd had a conversation with our family and decided that the time has come to sell the conference centre. We were just starting to pursue this. Then you call, out of the blue, and ask if we might consider selling part of the farm to A+! In short, we would indeed be willing to sell, but we'd be looking at the whole site including the conference centre and meeting halls, complete with the accommodation for 50, and our sports hall with the climbing wall you advised us to build!'

I did not know what to say. It would never have occurred to me to have had the audacity to suggest they move away and allow us to take over the wonderful conference centre they had built up over the past decade, as well as some adjoining land. But then I had no way of knowing that they were also feeling the time was right to move on.

Echoes of earlier adventures resonated somewhere in the recesses of my memory, and Steve Connor's advice: 'Mere coincidence, Jon. Don't let it build your faith!'

What an opportunity. What a challenge. What a concept!

Suddenly we were being offered the opportunity to create the Adventure*Base* we needed and to create a superb training and conference centre with an activity outlet, all on the same site. As I thought about what was being suggested I realised what a boost to our plans this would be.

I had envisaged trying to purchase a smallholding, with suitable land and maybe a cottage for our gap-year team to live in. This would have left us with the huge task of then raising funds to develop residential accommodation and facilities on site. We would also have the uphill struggle of trying to persuade the planning authority to allow us to develop a rural farm as an adventure and training centre.

But now here we were being offered a ready-made centre, with en-suite accommodation for 50, superb fully equipped commercial kitchens, training and conference facilities, including a cosy meeting room, complete with small kitchen and log burning stove, in a converted 16th-century Cotswold stone barn. There were even two beautiful Cotswold stone cottages on site – a marked improvement to our existing gap-year team accommodation.

And there was tremendous scope to develop an adventure centre just two fields away, on the same property!

It was both remote enough to allow adventure youth work without causing a disturbance to the conference centre or the village, and yet also right on the doorstop for adventure activities and training for guests at the conference centre.

It's all good for the humility. This is a far better plan than I would ever have envisaged.

This afternoon at 2 p.m., West Oxfordshire District Council will be considering an application for 'Change of Use of existing land and buildings' behind Windmill Farm Conference Centre, for use as the A+ Adventure*Base*.

For at least the next hour or two, the book will have to wait . . .

Result!

Four hours later, after much debate on miscellaneous local planning issues, the committee finally came round to discuss the application we were there to hear. We were almost last in the batting order so all but one of the public audience had left, leaving just Tessa and me at the front of the hall to hear the debate. We both found it hard not to intervene as various questions were asked of the senior planning officer about our plans for an Adventure*Base*.

Obviously we would have loved to explain the life-changing benefits to the thousands of young people who would be welcomed to the Adventure*Base* in the coming years, if only they could catch the vision and grant permission. In the event, we were hugely grateful for the testimonies of support for our work from among the planning committee and in the end the motion was carried with unanimous approval.

This was a major step forward in enabling us finally to bring to reality the vision we had first caught 25 years earlier: to provide a place where children and young people can be immersed in 'the serious business of having fun', in a positive Christian environment, and learn the eternal truth that they are greatly loved.

Bring it on! Now all we have to do is tie up the deal and find the money!

Bringing A+ Home

So here we are, 25 years on, with a thriving adventure company working with thousands of children every year. To all intents and purposes we've made it. Through a steady stream of amazing answers to prayer and a catalogue of adventures, Adventure*Plus* is certainly a 'happening' place to be.

I am often amazed by the impact our team has on visitors who come to visit us at our depot-HQ. I shouldn't be. Simply meeting the team, even just around the offices, makes a real impression on people, and that is not even when we are out in canoes, building woodland shelters or up on the hills. It is an immense privilege to work alongside this fine group of people that God has called to be part of his work at A+.

And yet . . . It certainly does not feel that we've arrived.

Our Biggest Challenge Yet

In many ways the challenges have just got a lot bigger. But with such an amazing story to look back on, and with the assurance from Malachi 3:6 ringing in our ears: 'I the Lord do not change,' we have confidence to face them.

And the big challenge ahead is, at least, easy to quantify. It comes in the shape and size of £1.3m to buy the property where we will build the Adventure*Base*. I am advised by people that know about money that this is a huge sum for an organisation our size. On paper we perhaps should not even be attempting it. We have been given 12 months to raise the first third of the money, a tidy £450,000, otherwise the property will go on sale on the open market.

If all goes well A+ will effectively take ownership of the land and we can move on site and make full use of it. We'll then have a further 12 months to raise the next £425,000, and another year to raise the remaining £425,000. Then the conference centre and Adventure*Base* land will finally be owned by Adventure*Plus* and secured for this work for generations to come. It's all very exciting. It is also very daunting from where I am sitting.

'His Ways Never Change'

As I was thinking and praying about this recently during a morning quiet time, I found myself wondering how on earth we were going to go about raising this kind of money. I have to confess I got distracted and turned to my phone!

I had just installed the BibleGateway App and decided to allow the distraction from my morning thought to run a little longer as I tried out the verse-search facility. For some reason the verse Philippians 4:18 came into my mind very clearly. It was a passage I did not know at all, but as that was the verse that kept coming to the fore in my mind I typed in 'Philippians 4:18'.

I read the verse, and then had to reread it to check I was not imagining it. Before I realised it I had read verse 19 too:

'And my God will meet all your needs according to the riches of his glory in Christ Jesus.'

We should not be surprised that even 25 years on and having worked with nearly 50,000 children and young people, the challenges are the same: to go where he calls and trust him to go ahead of us.

His ways 'do not change' (Malachi 3:6).

We just need to walk where he sends, and there is a clear sense here that God is enabling this next step. There is a door set open and we should walk through.

If you are reading this book in the first couple of years since it was published, we will doubtless be fully focused on working to raise the funds we will need to complete the purchase. If we have managed to do so by the time you read this, and A+ has secured the land, then I imagine we will be engaged in raising money to build the facilities on the land, to create the exciting Adventure*Base* that is already shaping up in our minds.

If you are reading some years from now, A+ could well be growing our vision of creating Adventure*Bases* in other areas of the UK, and maybe even overseas, to serve children and young people in other cities. It may be that you know someone who has land or buildings they would love to see used for this kind of outreach and encouragement to young people!

I do not expect the challenges to be any less once this project is established and children are being welcomed to our Adventure*Base* here in Oxfordshire.

God's Work, God's Way

It was the American evangelist and publisher in the 19th-century, D.L. Moody, who wrote:

'God's work, done God's way, will not lack God's resources.'

He found that to be true throughout his own adventures of faith and we are banking on it now as we move into this next phase of our adventure.

Is it a little rash to be taking our small organisation into such challenging and uncharted waters? If our experiences of the past 25 years are anything to go by, or D.L. Moody's or Hudson Taylor's 150 years ago . . . if the testimonies of thousands of believers across the centuries are to be believed . . . and if we allow ourselves to be strengthened by those wonderful words from Malachi, that 'God's ways never change . . .' and if we don't want to miss out on the next chapter of the adventure he has in store for us, and we remain eager to see how he plans to use it to bring encouragement to others for years to come . . . and if we don't want to find ourselves one day looking back on our lives and asking, 'What if I'd taken that next step?'. . . then we'd better pray, step up to the plate and get on with it!

And I hope one day you and many other readers will come and visit our Adventure*Base* and meet the amazing A+ team for yourself.

Epilogue

It is now 25 years since that conversation with the 23-year-old man who was already bored with life. Unknown to him, his comment 'There's got to be more to life than this!' had thrown out a huge challenge to me.

I am amazed as I look back over these pages to see how the adventure opened up, as we endeavoured to follow where that path has led. And yet the really exciting part of the story is of course yet to happen. We continue to work with a growing team of gifted adventure professionals committed to inspiring young people, whatever their background, to embrace the adventure of faith.

I cannot even begin to imagine the potential adventures that await the thousands of children and young people we work alongside each year, as they grow into the adventures he has in store for them. The potential for inspired and transformed lives is truly immeasurable.

It is an even more amazing thought for me as I sit here looking out at our autumn garden, that as you read this book, you may too decide to embrace the adventure of faith: look up and ask what adventures God has in store for you. We read in Jeremiah, God 'knows the plans he has for you . . . Plans to prosper and not to harm' (Jeremiah 29:11).

And I, for one, believe it.

Someone once shared with me a verse in the New Testament, which illuminates this invitation, this challenge to follow our own adventure. Ephesians 2:10 has become a favourite verse of mine as it captures the awesome thought that we are each created unique, with a different set of skills, and strengths and weaknesses. There are things in store for all of us, where the chemistry which makes up who we are, can be used to maximum benefit, for the good of others. And in doing what we can for others, we in turn are challenged and encouraged. And we stand to gain far more than we can ever give.

I think this is what Jesus meant when he said he came that we might 'have life, and have it to the full' (John 10:10). In seeking the best for others, which is of course at the heart of his teachings, we will in turn find we are also living 'Life to the max', as our A+ tee shirt puts it. Or, as Stewart, the Aussie Chef, inspired us to share with the children of the first school we ever worked with, 'Neighbours, everybody needs good neighbours!'

For some, this will involve pursuing excellence in the career or profession we feel called to or have been trained for. For others it will take us into an area for which we seem to have no experience or training. I certainly know that feeling. At times I've even felt like shouting out those immortalised words of the famous 1980s tennis champion, John McEnroe, when he disagreed with yet another umpire's decision: 'You cannot be serious!'

For many of us, if we're honest, the path ahead will at times seem overwhelmingly daunting. We may feel we just do not have what it takes to go there. When those feelings of doubt crowd our clarity and yet we still feel we should continue to seek that 'life in all its fullness', I remember that advice I was given at just such a time: 'God doesn't need our ability, he needs our availability.'

When I was 17 years old, my godmother sent me as a Christmas present a copy of *The Cross and the Switchblade* by David Wilkerson. It is the story of a country pastor in rural Pennsylvania who was reading the account in the papers of a gang in New York's Harlem ghetto who mugged and killed a disabled man in a wheelchair. The media sympathy was quite rightly with the victim, but David was surprised by a strong sense that he should visit the guys in prison and support them through the process of their trial and imprisonment.

The book goes on to relate the many adventures that David and his wife Gwen shared, as they followed the challenge that had been set before them. David's book is mirrored by an equally amazing account of the story told from the perspective of the gang leader, Nicky Cruz, in his book *Run Baby Run*, as he shares how he experienced for the first time, compassion and love from someone he did not even know – or like!

For me, the impact of these two books at that stage in my life was immense. If they were true, then they tell the story of a God who actually answers prayer, for real, in everyday life. I was just at that point when I was trying to decide which university course to apply for, or whether I should be aiming for something different, and I found myself struggling with the pointlessness of it all.

If all I was interested in was getting a well-paid job, and maybe marrying a beautiful girl and bringing up some fine kids, who hopefully would grow up to get a well-paid job, maybe marry beautiful people and have even more fine kids, then the whole process felt little more than an endless, point-less human conveyor belt. Much like my friend, I found myself asking 'What's the point?' I wanted to be part of something worthwhile, with a purpose, of lasting value.

Reading those books at that time really made an impact on me. 'If those books are true,' I thought, 'then God must be real, and if he is real, then I want to be part of his bigger picture'.

So one night I was surprised to find myself on my knees, saying a simple prayer: 'Dear God, if you are really there, then I want to be part of your bigger plan. Please show me what you want me to do?'

'Well,' I thought, 'if he isn't there, I've lost nothing, but if he is . . .'

I had two possible plans at the time, either to join the Royal Navy on a short service commission or to study nursing and work overseas for a couple of years. So I prayed earnestly for at least 10 minutes, which seemed much longer at the time, asking which of these two options I should take.

I half expected to see a vision of a warship ploughing through the high seas towards me, or maybe a syringe flying through the air . . . but I saw nothing. So after the 10 minutes I gave up, got into bed with, I am ashamed to admit, a sort of 'Well God, you've had your chance' kind of attitude.

It was at that point, when I least expected it, that I felt a sudden, deep and somehow warm assurance that I should go on to study nursing, and that this was the right path for me. This was to be the first step on a path that led eventually to the high adventure of our experience in Sudan, which led via some amazing God-incidences, some of which are shared in this book, to our present work with six thousand children and young people every year, and growing.

And the rest, as they say, is 'my story', and I have no doubt it was always 'his story' too, for my life. Well it's certainly an unfolding mystery, and it is at least part of my life's history!

As I sit here writing the closing page of this book, I am very aware that we have a team this afternoon out working with nearly fifty young people in Kent, and another team from A*im*, preparing to head up to North Oxfordshire, to work with about ten NEET young people from Banbury – if they show up. So our work continues here at A+, day by day, month by month.

What I am getting really excited about, however, is the next chapter. Not because I don't have to sit and write it, but because, if you are reading this book, then the next chapter is yours. Where will your adventure in faith take you? It need not involve international travel, or the kind of adventure youth work I was called to. You alone know the choices and opportunities that lie before you.

As a mountain leader I have learned that it is most important, on any journey, to know you are being led by a reliable guide, who knows the way, or at least that you are following a reliable map or guide book. Having read this far, I hope you will not mind me leaving you with probably my favourite verse, which is particularly relevant to the traveller who finds himself, or herself, at the point of decision:

'Stand at the crossroads and look;
Ask for the ancient paths,
Ask where the good way is, and walk in it
And you will find rest for your souls.'
(Jeremiah 6:16)

Stop, wait, ask, then walk . . . and you will one day be able to look back and say, 'I sought the good way and I followed where he sent.'

Of course, like me, you will never know what impact your decision to follow where he sends will have on the hundreds of lives you will have touched.

But that is their story . . . and is another part of his story! And the ongoing encouragements that will spin out from them are truly immeasurable.

SMILE

A+ is all about encouraging people to 'live the adventure of faith'.

If you have been inspired to seek out 'the good things he planned for us long ago' (Ephesians 2:10 NLT), or 'Life to the Max' (John 10:10 A+ style) we would love to hear from you.

Why not go to www.adventureplus.org.uk/SMILE to read what others have shared and to add your own testimony?*

It may just be that your experience will give others the confidence to stand for a while, ask where the good way is and even, perhaps, to walk in it . . .

*Why 'SMILE'?

I was with the family driving to a canoe trip in Wales and sharing the idea of a website where people can share their own encouragements and Emily piped up from the back seat of our people carrier:
'Great idea Dad, you should call it SMILE'
'Yep, I like that' I replied.
'No Dad, I haven't told you why yet: SMILE stands for Seeing Miracles In Life Everyday.'
'SMILE' – There's no better way to put it!

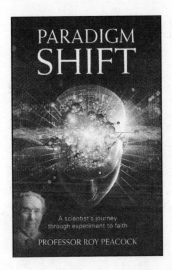

Paradigm Shift

A scientist's journey through experiment to faith

Roy Peacock

'No one sets out in life with the intention of becoming a thermodynamicist.'

Roy Peacock's life has been full of surprises. He planned to be an artist, but worked on aero engines; he was a religious sceptic, until the evidence supplied by his wife's conversion started a chain of events that led to his own; and he certainly didn't foresee his ministry of preaching and healing, which developed alongside his prestigious scientific career.

Paradigm Shift is a personal memoir of events which have shaped Roy's extraordinary life. It shows an experimental scientist testing the claims of the Bible in the same way he would any other truth claims, and finding that God acts as dramatically and speaks as clearly today as he did in Bible times. People are healed spiritually and physically as Roy increasingly learns to trust God in every area of his life.

978-1-78078-098-6

Runaway, Red Beret, and Reverend

The remarkable story of Mike Mcdade

Growing up in a broken home, Mike McDade decided he wanted to be rich and found his own dubious way of achieving this, despite leaving school with no qualifications and living on the streets. He had a Rolls Royce, a large house and holiday homes, yet, despite resisting at every turn, Mike left behind his flash lifestyle to become a Baptist minister. Mike has served in Bradford, Warrington (at the time of the IRA bomb attack), London and Cambridge and in each of these places he has left a deep impression. His unique life history had enabled him to get alongside and minister to those whom few others could reach.

Inspiring confirmation that God can help us to accomplish more than we can ask for or imagine.

978-1-78078-017-7

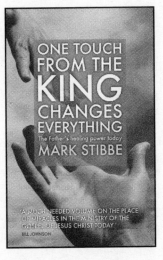

One Touch From the King Changes Everything

The Father's healing power today

Mark Stibbe

Mark Stibbe writes: 'Just one divine touch . . . that's all it takes.

'God can radically transform your situation with just one royal touch. A moment of divine contact can bring an invasion of heaven into your world. I believe with all my heart that Jesus can touch our lives today. When that happens, we see miracles.

'Healings can happen gradually; miracles happen instantly. Healings can involve a process; miracles involve a crisis. Healings can be partial; miracles are total. Healings can involve remissions; miracles involve cures.

'When I talk about "one touch from the King" I am referring to the gift of miracles – an instant, total, critical transformation. Don't you long for that kind of manifestation today?'

978-1-86024-810-8

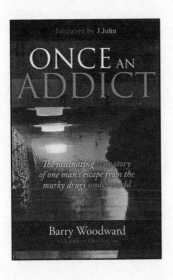

Once an Addict

*The fascinating true story
of one man's escape from
the murky drugs
underworld*

*Barry Woodward
with Andrew Chamberlain*

Barry Woodward was a drug dealer and heroin addict who once lived on the notorious Bull Rings in the centre of Manchester. *Once an Addict* describes Barry's descent into the murky underworld of drug dealing, addiction, crime and imprisonment. Along the way we are introduced to some of the most extraordinary characters, and we see the extreme lengths to which some of them will go to get their next 'fix'. Illegal drug use claimed the lives of many such people, and it seemed inevitable that Barry would also succumb to the consequences of his addiction.

Wth devastating amphetimine-induced mental health issues, a fourteen-year heroin addiction, a string of broken relatonships, and the threat of HIV looming, the outlook for Barry appeared very bleak. Then three extraordinary encounters changed his live forever . . .

978-1-86024-602-9

Authentic

We trust you enjoyed reading this book
from Authentic Media. If you want to be
informed regarding the next publication from this
author and other exciting releases you can sign up
to the Authentic newsletter online:

www.authenticmedia.co.uk

Contact us:

By Post:
Authentic Media
52 Presley Way
Crownhill
Milton Keynes
MK8 0ES

E-mail:
info@authenticmedia.co.uk

Follow us: